Understanding assessment and qualifications in post-compulsory education and training

Principles, politics and practice

SECOND EDITION

Understanding assessment and qualifications in post-compulsory education and training

Principles, politics and practice

SECOND EDITION

Kathryn Ecclestone

niace
promoting adult learning

promoting adult learning

21 De Montfort Street
Leicester
LE1 7GE

Company registration no. 2603322
Charity registration no. 1002775

Reprinted 2006

NIACE has a broad remit to promote lifelong learning
opportunities for adults. NIACE works to develop
increased participation in education and training,
particularly for those who do not have easy access
because of class, gender, age, race, language and culture,
learning difficulties or disabilities, or insufficient
financial resources.

You can find NIACE online at www.niace.org.uk

Cataloguing in Publication Data
A CIP record of this title is available from the British Library

Designed and typeset by Avon DataSet Ltd, Bidford on Avon, B50 4JH
Print and bound in the UK by Biddles Limited

ISBN: 978 1 86201 234 9

Contents

ASSESSMENT AND QUALIFICATIONS IN LIFELONG LEARNING

Recognising why assessment is becoming more important

Assessment and formal processes to recognise and certificate achievements now dominate all the diverse sectors that comprise post-compulsory education and training. Yet the growing importance of assessment and certification over the past 20 years has also revealed conflicting educational and political ideas about what counts as 'achievement', how best to motivate learners and how to ensure 'fair' assessment. Support for assessment systems that are flexible, accessible and able to recognise diverse achievements exists in parallel with growing political concern about quality assurance, the accountability of education providers and the maintenance of standards of achievement across very diverse sectors of post-16 education and training. The remit of the Learning and Skills Council (LSC) to oversee post-16 education and training outside higher education, together with the introduction in 2003 of an inspection regime for adult and community education, increases these pressures.

At the same time, numerous attempts since the early 1980s to rationalise the UK's assessment and qualifications system have not worked. A complex system of credits, certification processes, quality assurance and qualifications, offered by hundreds of awarding bodies, continues to confuse the public, practitioners, institution managers, inspectors and LSC officials alike. Not only is the structure of the qualifications system complex, with diverse agencies and interest groups involved in design, implementation and quality assurance, but changes have not been accompanied by coherent professional development to help practitioners makes sense of it all. In addition, political and educational tensions underly apparently straightforward practical injunctions for practitioners to use

1

assessment in order to raise standards, motivate more learners to achieve and to promote the skills for lifelong learning. As a result, assessment is problematic for qualification designers, inspectors, managers of educational programmes, practitioners and learners.

As well as developments in qualifications, a series of political initiatives and requirements from external bodies during the 1980s and 1990s have had a significant impact on how learners and practitioners regard the purposes of assessment and on how institutions organise and offer different assessment practices. These initiatives include:

- national targets for achievement of qualifications at different levels, together with targets for participation and retention in formal education and training and for participation in informal learning;
- new arrangements for inspection in further education colleges, work-based training providers and adult and community education, carried out by the Office for Standards in Education (OfSTED) and the Adult Learning Inspectorate (ALI), alongside new arrangements for quality assurance carried out by the local LSCs and awarding bodies;
- the development of ideas and activities for measuring 'soft' learning outcomes;
- a growth in opportunities for learners to gain credit for individual units or modules in more flexible combinations, to accumulate these over time and to transfer them between different education and training programmes;
- the steady increase in initiatives to specify detailed learning outcomes, assessment criteria and 'quality standards' as the basis for designing, teaching and assessing learning programmes;
- new attempts by the Qualifications and Curriculum Authority (QCA) to use assessment models in order to harmonise different qualifications and certificates within a national qualifications framework.

Making assessment more educational

Political imperatives are not the only reason for taking assessment more seriously and understanding its implications. There is growing research evidence that when assessment systems are used well, they can play a powerful and positive role in motivating learners and encouraging them to take more control over their learning. The idea that assessment is integral to effective learning and motivation underpins attempts to maximise the educational benefits of assessment and to clarify its different purposes. This interest, together with attempts to make post-16 assessment systems both inclusive and motivating, have been influenced strongly by vocational initiatives throughout the 1980s and 1990s to encourage young people to stay on in formal education. During the same period, similar objectives underpinned moves to develop outcome-based models of assessment and to assess and accredit 'prior learning' for adults in order to encourage more adults to progress from informal to formal learning (see UDACE, 1994).

These initiatives reflect a broader shift from norm-referenced systems that were based on the enduring idea, peculiar to the UK and particularly to England, that assessment must select those learners with 'innate ability' for limited places in education and a limited supply of good jobs. Norm-referencing, psychometric testing and selection based on intelligence tests have created a strong cultural legacy for our education system. This influences technical systems and practices within various assessment models and creates populist images of assessment particularly in relation to images of intelligence, ability and standards, particularly in relation to images of intelligence, ability and standards (see Broadfoot, 1996 for discussion).

In contrast, criterion-referenced and outcome-based systems aim to encourage people's potential, to recognise diverse forms of achievement, to base progression on merit, to make practitioners and institutions more accountable and to promote learner autonomy. In outcome-based assessment models, such goals depend on giving people access to public specifications of outcomes and criteria. In theory at least, this not only encourages learners to engage more actively with assessment but also makes evidence of achievement more flexible and therefore less dependent on formal structures and syllabi. The notion of flexibility also makes accumulation and transfer of formal credit and certification possible, together with accreditation of prior achievement in formal learning programmes (see Jessup, 1991; McNair, 1995).

The political and educational aims of assessment in these approaches resonate with growing interest amongst academic and policy-based researchers in the potential power of formative and diagnostic assessment to raise standards of attainment, to motivate learners and to make them more autonomous as learners. In part, current research around these goals builds upon initiatives in the 1980s to promote portfolios and records of achievement (see Broadfoot, 1986; Wolf, 1998). More broadly, research evidence shows that better diagnosis of learners' needs and interests, reviews of achievement and involving learners actively in assessing the quality of their work, are all integral to progressive assessment. A key goal in this research is to create 'communities of practice' between practitioners and learners. These communities are based on developing shared understandings of criteria for quality and accompanying processes to use these criteria as a basis for dialogue about achievement (see Gipps, 1994; Black and Wiliam, 1998).

Understanding confusion

More broadly, long-term demographic and structural changes in the job market are leading to pressures on the education and training system to attract and retain new groups of learners. Almost eighty per cent of young people now stay on in full-time education at 16 and formal education and assessment structures are extending into work-based learning for adults, as well as into adult and community education. The percentage of adults in higher education has increased over 15 years to over 30 per cent, many of whom are part-time. One effect of a rise in participation across the post-compulsory system is the formalisation of assessment and quality-assurance systems. This blurs distinctions between assessment systems for 16 to 19 year olds and adult returners. More adults and young people are now assessed for some form of certification and this has led to attempts to standardise assessment methods and systems across the education and training system. Political targets for achievement put further pressure on forms of assessment that are responsive to learners in very different contexts of education. As a result, assessment systems become more standardised in formats that recognise achievement in easily quantifiable outcomes and are used to evaluate whether national targets have been met and for inspecting the quality of teaching and learning activities.

These changes make it important to place current approaches and debates within a broader history of assessment. This shows that political and social goals for education affect aspirations for what assessment can do for individuals and for society as a whole at different points in history (see Gipps, 1995; Broadfoot, 1996). As formal assessment becomes more prominent in post-16 education and training, more groups have a vested interest in its outcomes and the ways it is managed, both in and between institutions. Different interests are evident, for example, in debates about what educational standards really signify. Competing political and educational interests are also evident in debates about 'parity of esteem' between traditional forms of assessment and newer approaches. Tension over both parity and status of qualifications arises from an emphasis in the past on selecting people for rationed places in higher education, based on psychometric testing and norm-referencing, and a corresponding belief that assessment can measure and predict people's intelligence. In contrast, there is growing interest in assessment that can provide authentic and rich accounts of people's achievements, both for formal recognition and confidence building, and for certification towards qualifications.

These tensions are complex and far from easy to resolve, either politically or technically. They make it difficult for practitioners and learners to recognise different principles and purposes of assessment. It is also difficult to translate some of these principles into worthwhile assessment for learning and then into valid and reliable accounts of achievement. From a technical perspective, most practitioners regard the processes of designing and awarding qualifications as the responsibility of awarding bodies and their officials. Despite the influence of bodies such as the Open College Networks in involving teachers and institutions actively in curriculum development, teaching and certification of achievements, many practitioners and learners are unclear about how formative, diagnostic and summative assessment fit into curriculum and course design and teaching and learning. Differences between formative assessment to enhance learning and summative assessment for certification are exacerbated by a strong emphasis on inspection and quality assurance on summative outcomes and targets. Such tensions undermine the potential of formative assessment to enhance learning and can lead to over-compliance with procedures to get through the summative demands of a qualification.

Post-16 practitioners and tutors also tend to be familiar with the traditions and ethos of the particular assessment and qualifications systems they use with learners. One effect is that they might not make connections between these systems in terms of broader principles and purposes. Inside institutions, this can lead to confusion about different awarding body requirements and duplication of systems for quality assurance. This is especially true in colleges that deal with a large number of awarding bodies. It is therefore important to connect the various quality control and quality assurance procedures that different bodies use in terms of teachers' understanding of them. In addition, the evolution of *ad hoc* arrangements, often in response to different educational policies and initiatives at different times, together with repeated restructuring of the post-16 sector itself, have resulted in partial knowledge of assessment issues within awarding bodies, the QCA, post-16 inspectorates and the LSC.

Being more strategic about assessment

Changes to structures in the post-16 system have compounded technical barriers to understanding assessment and qualifications. The Learning and Skills sector is extraordinarily complicated. It brings new agencies and organisations into local and national partnerships, many of whom have very different traditions and expectations of assessment and who may not understand the role of other organisations. It is therefore important to identify these agencies and to understand their links with each other.

Understanding some of the political, educational and technical complexities of assessment is especially important now that educational organisations have to raise achievement and motivation amongst 14 and 16 year olds and adults across diverse sectors of learning. A better understanding is also important because there is a growing harmonisation of goals and models for assessment from General Certificates of Secondary Education (GCSEs), Advanced Vocational and General Qualifications (A-levels), university degrees and assessment in adult and community education. This will gain momentum as proposals from the Tomlinson Committee on 14–19 reform are translated into new systems for assessment.

Another reason to be more strategic about assessment arises because initiatives to widen participation, raise achievement and improve retention, and to motivate non-traditional learners in formal learning programmes, tend to promote outdated images of adult learners. This means that adults' needs for assessment are likely to change rapidly: as increasing numbers of young people who experience assessment after compulsory schooling become adult returners later on, they will be familiar with assessment systems within different qualifications and have particular expectations about them. One effect is that a strong contemporary image of the uncertain, under-confident adult returner who fears traditional forms of assessment is likely to have less resonance over time.

Recognising controversial aspects of assessment

Great emphasis on assessment in schools affects attitudes to assessment and learning in post-compulsory education and training. For example, negative effects of formal assessment on motivation and ideas about learning in the National Curriculum for schools and in further and higher education may create new forms of disaffection about the demands of summative assessment and testing. There is evidence, for example, of growing compliance and low-risk approaches amongst National Curriculum pupils and post-16 learners (see, for example, Pollard and Broadfoot, 2000; Ecclestone, 2002). Expectations of assessment instilled through compulsory schooling place new demands on post-16 practitioners and institutions to use assessment imaginatively as well as strategically.

As well as technical complexity and confusion over basic principles and activities, assessment in post-16 education and training has become controversial. The burden of assessment in outcome-based models such as National Vocational Qualifications (NVQs) and General National Vocational Qualifications (GNVQs) (now Advanced Vocational Certificates in Education (AVCEs)), for example, has caused confusion amongst assessors in workplaces and education institutions. Outcome-based models have obscured the links between assessment and learning (see Hyland, 1994; Ecclestone, 2002 for discussion). These problems are compounded by the way that policy-makers use outcome-based assessment systems for funding decisions, judgements about organisational performance and ideas about what counts as achievement based on assessment outcomes. Indeed, 'learning' has become synonymous with achievement of quantifiable targets, leading to new meanings of 'participation in learning' and 'non-learners'.

The complexities and controversies outlined here make it important to appreciate the underlying principles of assessment, the politics that affect how these principles are translated into practice and the resulting effects on everyday assessment activities between both practitioners and learners and practitioners and external agencies. Such complexity can also make practitioners and policy-makers in Britain (and particularly in England) peculiarly ethnocentric: we tend to overlook how developments in the UK, although often very different in ethos and practice from developments in other European countries, can sometimes also be very similar.

Following arguments so far, it seems that education and training providers need to simultaneously adopt a more strategic, analytical and critical approach to providing different assessment services and activities for learners and to providing evidence for quality assurance to external bodies such as LSCs, inspectorates and awarding bodies.

This book

As part of a response to the issues outlined here, this book aims to cut through some of the complexity by relating basic principles and practices of post-16 assessment to some of the broader developments in qualification systems. It also highlights some tensions and controversies that these developments and practices reflect. The book draws extensively on research into assessment and quality assurance in further, adult and higher education and from research that has arisen from my own participation between 1997–2002 in a group of European vocational education researchers in assessment and evaluation and in a research project over the past four years with the National Board of Education in Finland. Importantly, too, ideas in the book are influenced strongly by research and development activities with post-16 practitioners and trainers who study principles, policy and practice in assessment as part of continuing professional development programmes at the university where I work, and by my research activities between 1999 and 2003 with two major awarding bodies, namely City & Guilds and NCFE (an awarding body in further, adult and community education), between 1999 and 2002.

This book aims to:
- clarify different terms, principles, purposes and practices involved in assessment and the quality assurance procedures within different qualifications;
- highlight the main tensions that make these processes problematic, particularly for institutional managers, practitioners and tutors trying to implement policy injunctions;
- offer some practical strategies for improving assessment practices and processes associated with accreditation;
- suggest other literature and research that might be useful as follow-up reading for practical and theoretical insights; and
- raise the level of debate between and within institutions and government agencies about the best ways of providing assessment and about the underlying purposes of different assessment activities offered to learners.

A note about purpose and audience

Some of the book updates and extends two earlier publications, 'Understanding Assessment' and 'Understanding Accreditation', published in

1994 by NIACE and the Further Education Unit (now the Learning and Skills Development Agency) respectively. One assumption reflected in both these publications almost ten years ago was that practitioners need and can learn from direct guidance and explanation.

Although there is a place for technical guidance and explanation, these earlier publications reflected a growing tendency in official reports and guidance to practitioners and institutional managers for what might be called 'death by a thousand bullet points', where very complex ideas, dilemmas and value judgments in education were distilled into unproblematic lists. This approach is not only tedious to read and engage with, but is also very limited in terms of its educational possibilities.

In contrast, I have attempted here to combine didactic explanation with explicit acknowledgement of problematic areas of policy, theory and practice and to indicate further reading where these deeper issues are explored. By doing this, the book aims to show how some of the underlying principles of assessment, together with their implementation in different assessment systems, reflect conflicts in educational values as well as political manipulation and unanticipated negative effects. Tensions and areas of controversy are highlighted at the end of each chapter, and in the discussion of standards in Chapter Two and of autonomy and motivation in Chapter Four.

Each chapter also offers ideas for further reading in the form of annotated references. These combine the technical texts of official agencies, government departments and awarding bodies with academic articles and books that aim to be more critical, wide-ranging and reflective. Hopefully, then, the bullet points that *do* appear in parts of the book become useful summaries of points rather than a substitute for explanation or reflection about ideas.

Professional educators are more deluged by official guidance, accounts of 'best practice' and evaluations of their activities by external agencies than ever before. This means that motivation to consider how assessment raises questions about our educational and social beliefs and values may be at a premium. Nevertheless, while tensions and controversies might seem to be a recurring theme in the book, the intention is to expose them in order to try to find political and professional solutions, rather than to assume that yet more technical clarification is the answer.

For simplicity, the book uses the term 'learners' to encompass students, trainees and participants, and 'practitioners' to encompass teachers, tutors, advisers, lecturers and trainers. I do recognise, however, that the roles that practitioners and learners in different contexts adopt, or are asked to take on, reflect important differences in ethos, identity and activity. The book also focuses more on assessment in educational institutions and providers than on workplaces, although the ideas discussed throuhout the book are relevant to all contexts where assessment takes place.

Those who might find the book useful include:

- assessment officers in awarding bodies who are new to their post;
- programme and curriculum managers in further education colleges, adult education providers and universities;
- staff development officers;
- lecturers, tutors, advisors and trainers working with assessment systems;
- inspectors;
- trainee tutors, lecturers and teachers.

The structure of the book:

Chapter One explores different purposes for assessment and clarifies its diagnostic, formative and summative functions. The chapter shows that *methods* of assessment do not characterise them as diagnostic, formative or summative: instead, methods can achieve different aims, depending largely on the purpose and audience for assessment. The chapter also summarises different types of assessment, namely *norm-referencing, criterion-referencing* and *ipsative (self-referencing)* assessment.

Chapter Two clarifies key principles of assessment such as validity, reliability and authenticity. It relates these terms to methods that aim to fulfil different principles, such as outcome-based assessment versus examinations, or records of achievement. It also contrasts some of the shifts in principles, evident in the rise of outcome-based assessment systems and records of achievement in the 1980s and 1990s, with new emphasis in post-16 qualifications policy on external tests.

Chapter Three describes and evaluates the links between formative and diagnostic assessment and learning. It highlights barriers to realising the potential of formative and diagnostic assessment to enhance learning and motivation. It also indicates some practical strategies to try and realise these aims.

Chapter Four considers what motivation and autonomy mean in outcome-based assessment systems. Discussion in this chapter extends some of the ideas in Chapter Three about the links between assessment and learning.

Chapter Five analyses key features of quality assurance in different qualifications. It defines terms such as *validation, moderation, verification, quality assurance* and *quality control*. This chapter aims to clarify procedures so that practitioners understand the roles of awarding body officials, examination boards and inspectors.

Chapter Six offers ideas about developing an organisational assessment policy. This enables education institutions, teams and individual practitioners to consider what this might encompass and to plan a programme of staff development in assessment.

References and further reading

Accounts of the changing social and educational roles of assessment and qualifications in the UK

Broadfoot, P. (1986) *Education, Assessment and Society: a sociological analysis*. Buckingham: Open University Press.

Young, M. (1998) *The Curriculum of the Future*. London: Falmer Press.

Young, M. (2002) 'Contrasting approaches to the role of qualifications in the promotion of lifelong learning' in Evans, K., Hodkinson, P. and Unwin, L. (eds) (2002) *Working to Learning: transforming learning in the workplace*. London: Kogan Page.

A critique of the effects of the drive in current policy towards certification in post-16 education and training

Ainley, P. (1999) *Learning Policy: Towards the Certified Society*. Basingstoke: Macmillan Press.

Theoretical analysis and discussion of the policy and practice implications of developing more effective approaches to formative and diagnostic assessment

Black, P. and Wiliam, D. (1998a) *Inside the Black Box: Raising Standards Through Classroom Assessment*, Occasional Paper. School of Education, King's College London.

Black, P. and Wiliam, D. (1998b) 'Assessment and classroom learning: Assessment' in *Education: Principles, Policy and Practice*, 5, 1, 1–78.

Gipps, C. (1994) *Beyond Testing: Towards a Theory of Educational Assessment*. London: Falmer Press.

Discussion of the principles and goals of records of achievement and outcome-based assessment

Broadfoot, P. (1998) 'Records of achievement and the learning society: a tale of two discourses: Assessment' in *Education: Principles, Policy and Practice*, 5, 3, 413–447.

Burke, J. (ed.) (1995) *Outcomes Learning and the Curriculum: Implications for NVQs GNVQs and Other Qualifications*. London: Falmer Press.

Jessup, G. (1991) *Outcomes: NVQs and the emerging model of education and training*. London: Falmer.

McNair, S. (1995) 'Outcomes and autonomy' in Burke, J. (ed.) (1995): *Outcomes, Learning and the Curriculum: Implications for NVQs, GNVQs and other qualifications*. London: Falmer Press.

Otter, S. (1989) *Understanding Learning Outcomes*. Leicester: Unit for the Development of Adult and Continuing Education.

UDACE (1994) *Learning Outcomes in Higher Education*. London: UDACE/Further Education Unit.

Practical guides to defining and assessing learning outcomes in adult and community education

Foster, P., Howard, U. and Reisenberger, A. (1997) *A sense of achievement: outcomes of adult learning*. London: Further Education Development Agency.

Greenwood, M., Hayes, A., Turner, C. and Vorhaus, J. (eds) (2001) *Recognising and validating outcomes of non-accredited learning: a practical approach*. London: Further Education Development Agency.

Analysis and critique of the impact of assessment on learning

Broadfoot, P. and Pollard, A. (2000) 'The changing discourse of assessment policy: the case of English primary education' in Filer, A.(ed.) (2000): *Assessment: Social Process, Social Product*. London: Falmer Press.

Ecclestone, K. (2002) *Learning Autonomy in Post-16 Education: the policy and practice of formative assessment*. London: Routledge/Falmer Press.

Filer, A. (ed.) (2000) *Assessment: Social Process, Social Product*. London: Falmer Press.

Hyland, T. (1994) *Competence, Education and NVQs*. London: Cassell.

CHAPTER 1

THE PURPOSES OF ASSESSMENT

Introduction

Over the past 20 years, the design and content of qualifications in the post-14 curriculum, higher education degrees and adult and community education have shown a marked political and social shift. Broadly, this has been from assessment for selection for employment, licences to practise a profession and progression in further and higher education, towards assessment designed to enhance motivation and generic learning skills (often referred to as 'learning to learn') and to provide a more authentic basis for certifying work-related competence.

Whatever its purpose, assessment drives curriculum content and perceptions among learners, practitioners and funders about what is important in a learning programme. For example, 'teaching to the test' might induce learners to become either strategically compliant and to adopt superfical or surface approaches to learning and to reject deep engagement. However, if the test is well designed, teaching to it might also promote deep engagement with a range of important skills and attitudes. The content, design and goals of any test or assessment method therefore exert a huge influence on what learners and practitioners regard as important. Where tests or assignments emphasise results or learning outcomes that enable external agencies to measure and compare institutions, they are more likely to induce undesirable compliance and low-level engagement than if they aim to assess authentic, real-life skills. The problem is that the more complex the skills being assessed, the less amenable the methods are as a basis for measuring and comparing institutions.

Further pressures on types of assessment arise from the way that government, funding agencies and inspectors increasingly use the outcomes of assessment for league tables, performance targets and funding decisions. While there is potential for assessment to have positive effects on learning, there is a strong tendency for final or end assessment, and its uses for progression to the next stage (employment or more formal education), to dominate our images of assessment. In post-compulsory education, different qualifications and courses use different methods. For example, certification may depend on methods for accumulating evidence from assignments and activities against pre-defined statements of competence or achievement. In other contexts, final assessment hinges on end examinations, based perhaps on an unseen paper or on multiple choice tests. There may also be oral presentations, an interview or a learning diary.

The use of a range of methods tends to obscure the fact that any method can be used for quite different purposes. In addition, a need to guide practitioners and managers through the requirements of diverse and often changing qualification systems has produced more prescriptive assessment regimes and official guidance. In many cases, this top-down advice and regulation replaces staff induction or opportunities for professional development around assessment issues.

As assessment systems continue to evolve to meet different, even competing purposes in the UK's education and training system, the tension between assessment for testing and assessment for learning increases. In the light of this problem, this chapter:

- defines 'assessment';
- identifies different purposes of assessment;
- highlights some important types of assessment; and
- offers a framework within which educational institutions can plan assessment activities.

1. Purposes of assessment

Broadly, there are four main reasons for assessing learners, no matter what type of programme they are following. Assessment can be used by learners and practitioners to:

- diagnose strengths and weaknesses and learning needs for the forthcoming programme;
- provide feedback on progress, strengths and weaknesses and barriers to learning, as a basis for setting targets and designing learning and assessment activities;
- select learners for the next educational stage, such as the next module, a new programme, progression to another institution or level, or for work; and
- certificate and confirm achievements to a wider audience, such as employers and admissions tutors at the next stage of progression.

Each of these purposes requires assessment activities to produce different information in different formats. Each purpose also has a specific audience in terms of *users* of assessment and *stakeholders* interested in its quality and cost-effectiveness. These include government agencies such as the Qualifications and Curriculum Authority, awarding bodies and inspectorates, employers, admissions tutors in further and higher education, practitioners, parents and, of course, learners themselves. In addition, the outcomes of assessment for selection and certification form the basis for official evaluation and inspection.

Diagnosis

Assessment to diagnose needs for learning can be used primarily for learners and their practitioners, or for external audiences. For the first audience, it underpins teaching and learning activities by building upon previous experience and achievements and helping someone to identify next steps. Diagnostic assessment can therefore take place at different stages of a learning programme but important features include:
- offering initial guidance and advice;
- establishing strategies and habits that learners have in relation to study and other learning activities;
- providing regular tutorial support and reviews of progress;
- using feedback from teaching and marking coursework and assignments; and
- providing information for other practitioners and assessors in learners' programmes.

Feedback

Inextricably linked to diagnosis, assessment can provide timely and constructive feedback on learners' progress. This helps learners identify where their progress and achievements lie in relation to the summative criteria for assessment: what Sadler calls 'closing the gap' between where someone is during different points of a learning programme and the standard of achievement they will need to attain by the end (1989). Clear criteria, reviews of progress and learners' active engagement with feedback are all integral to its effectiveness.

Selection and recruitment

Although many institutions or organisations aim to be flexible and accessible in attracting new learners and helping them to achieve, processes for entry to programmes nearly always require some form of assessment. Admissions tutors, employers and course leaders therefore use assessment to:

- recruit people to jobs by specifying particular qualifications or grades;
- admit learners to learning programmes by publishing different entry requirements;
- select people to practise a trade or profession by requiring specific types of membership examinations or previous work experiences; and
- select employees for promotion or in-service training/development.

Certificating achievements

Evidence of achievement, whether from a portfolio of coursework or written examinations, provides confirmation of someone's skills, attributes and qualities. In some professions or crafts, assessment confers an official licence to practice. This confirmation is open to public and political evaluation and is therefore a particular focus for inspectors and funding bodies as a measurement of quality. The outcomes of summative assessment appear increasingly in institutional league tables. Assessment therefore:

- provides information about progress towards national targets for participation, retention and achievement;
- enables funding bodies to make decisions about levels of funding;
- provides information for league tables; and
- fuels debates about rising or falling standards and the respective merits of different types of learning programmes.

Assessment is therefore carried out on behalf of diverse interested groups, in different sectors and stages of education and training, to achieve a number of purposes or functions. It might be helpful to see assessment as something that is able to answer different questions, as shown in Figure 1.

Figure 1 Questions that assessment can answer for different audiences

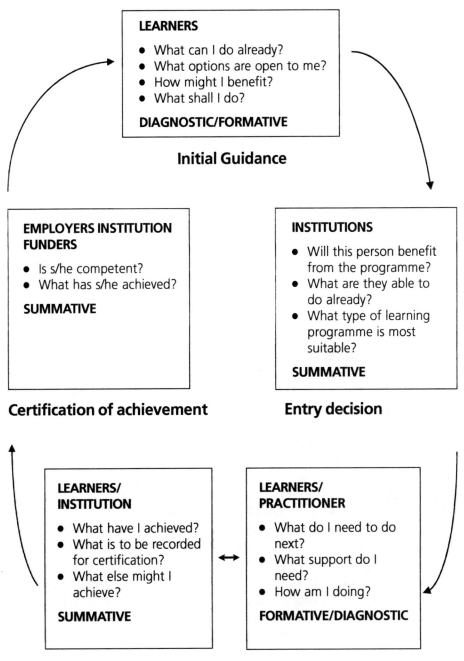

2. Types of assessment

A definition of assessment

In order to achieve the different purposes of assessment outlined so far, it is important to clarify what all assessment activities have in common. Assessment involves a judgement of evidence for a particular purpose, and uses a standard or scale for making that judgement. Some assessment has very explicit and formalised definitions of what constitutes appropriate achievement, such as NVQs or GNVQs, while other assessment is more informal with vague or implicit definitions of the standard. Standards or scales therefore take many forms but applying them involves measuring the individual against one of three things:

- an absolute criterion (can this person add two plus two to make four/carry out a procedure with 100% accuracy etc.) (criterion-referencing);
- performance of a cohort or group (can this person do this task better or worse than his or her cohort/this year's Maths candidates/all mathematicians) (norm-referencing); and
- the learner's own previous performance (can this person do this better than they could last week?) (ipsative).

Different purposes of assessment

Although the purposes of assessment are closely linked, they are often confused in actual practice. It is therefore important to be as precise as possible about which purpose an assessment activity is designed to fulfil at a particular time in a person's learning programme.

Formative assessment is carried out for practitioners and learners. It is associated with diagnosing learners' needs, their previous achievements, the barriers they might have to different aspects of learning, their strengths and weaknesses, and the strategies and approaches they tend to adopt. It therefore requires effective strategies for diagnosing needs, giving feedback on achievement and enabling learners to engage actively with these processes (see Chapter Three for further discussion of links between assessment and learning).

Summative assessment is carried out on behalf of employers, higher and further education institutions, professional bodies and the funding councils. It provides publicly accountable confirmation of achievements so that learners can progress to the next stage – a job, further or higher education, a new module, the next level. It is therefore a formal process of certificating achievements and is associated with grading, accountability and public results.

Formative assessment can be formal and carried out strategically so that practitioners plan for it to happen, or it can take place informally and in more *ad hoc* ways during teaching, tutorials and reviews. Formative assessment is often used informally (but not always effectively!) when learners assess their own work or that of friends. Processes of self and peer assessment can therefore be informal and *ad hoc* or more strategic and formal. It is important to adopt a more conscious use of such approaches in order to increase their effectiveness in providing formative feedback.

In contrast, summative assessment is always formal and is usually carried out for more than one external audience, such as an awarding body, admissions tutors, employers, funding bodies and inspectors. Most people associate assessment with its summative purposes and tend to overlook its formative potential. Following the distinctions made here, any method can be used summatively or formatively: for example, a written test can be used formatively – to diagnose skills or attributes and then plan appropriate learning activities – or summatively.

Different types of assessment

Formative and summative assessment both use some form of criteria or standards for measurement. These might be explicit and presented in public documents or explained to learners by practitioners, or they can be implicit and held in the minds of practitioners and examiners and not communicated overtly to learners. The criteria might also be informal and negotiable between practitioners and learners, or formal and prescribed by awarding bodies. However, the distinction is not entirely clear-cut: criteria might be quite formal yet still have scope for negotiation, or be informal and prescriptive.

Generally, criteria or standards for measurement may be explicitly or implicitly based on:

- general notions of how an 'excellent', 'average' or 'poor' learner in a particular age group or stage of learning performs (norm-referencing);
- direct comparisons with other learners in the same group or cohort (norm-referencing);
- an absolute, externally defined measure or standard (criterion-referencing); or
- a learner's own previous performance (self-referencing or 'ipsative assessment').

Norm-referencing

Norm-referencing derives assessment criteria from the norms of achievement set by other learners. These norms might be based on general notions of how other 'excellent', 'average' or 'poor' learners perform, or direct comparisons with other learners in the same group or annual cohort, or between cohorts over a period of time. It is possible to differentiate between 'hard' systems of norm-referencing that have technical processes that standardise and rank student performance in relation to the highest and lowest level of attainment shown by other candidates, and 'soft', more general applications of norm-referencing. Confusion arises because some form of norm-referencing underpins the ways in which institutions, employers and awarding bodies compare one year's performance with that of previous cohorts in order to evaluate standards. Concerns about rising or falling standards, evident each year when A-level and GCSE results come out, reflect aspects of a norm-referenced tradition.

In norm-referenced systems, then, an individual's achievement is measured in comparison to:

- peers from a learner's class or group;
- a wider group of candidates, such as the annual regional, local or national group undertaking the assessment;
- historical data from a particular cohort over a period of time.

In broad terms, norm-referencing aims to:

- enable educational institutions and employers to select people where there is competition for limited places;
- allow practitioners and examiners to rank learners in order of performance;
- provide a statistical basis for distributing marks (for example, ten per cent gaining the highest, ten per cent failing and the rest gaining a grade in between these two; this can create a 'normal curve of distribution' across the range of available grades;
- enable external bodies to compare the relative performance of learners over a period of time.

Norm-referencing may have a legitimate role, or affect assessment formally and informally when:

- demand for access to places exceeds the number on offer or there is pressure on resources for selection and admissions processes;
- employers, parents and other interested groups wish to quickly compare standards of performance between learners through the use of league tables;

- criteria for assessment are not debated between practitioners or shared between learners;
- test designers use notions of a 'typical' learner in setting tests and assessment tasks and practitioners mark learners' work by setting the 'best' and 'worst' standard in the group for high and low marks;
- practitioners use images of 'high' and 'low' ability when describing learners and the quality of their work.

Norm-referencing may be based on pre-determined criteria but these often rely on implicit notions of good/excellent/poor performance. In 'hard' norm-referenced systems, criteria are not made explicit to learners, and awarding or examining bodies devise mechanisms to make interpretations of criteria consistent between examiners. The actual level or standard of achievement gained for the top and failure mark can also vary with each cohort since the overall aim is to produced a standardised level of achievement within each cohort. Information about rank order is therefore much more important to end-users of assessment in this system than details of individual achievements or how these were gained.

Recent uses of assessment and qualifications to open up access to learning opportunities and to motivate learners have led to a widely held view that norm-referenced assessment has negative educational and social effects. Criticisms arise from a number of features:

- criteria for comparing learners are often based on tacit or implicit notions amongst practitioners and examiners about what constitutes good or poor performance;
- these criteria are rarely shared between practitioners, examiners and learners, so that learners do not know quite how their performance will be judged;
- the actual level or standard of achievement for the top and the failure mark varies each year between different cohorts, resulting in a complex process of adjusting the distribution of marks;
- information about the grade and rank order dominates practitioners' and learners' perceptions about what is important in the learning process and downplays the importance of individuals' achievements or how they gained them;

Over the past twenty years, there has been a concerted move away from norm-referencing towards the use of external measures and criteria. In spite of this, social, political and educational pressures can exert a strong pull back towards norm-referencing in some assessment systems and qualifications. Disagreement about whether vocational A-levels (AVCEs) are equivalent to general A-levels, for example, is partly because their predecessor, General National Vocational Qualifications (GNVQs), did not use norm-referenced grading, thereby making it difficult to construct league table comparisons of grades.

Criterion-referencing

The growth in the educational and political popularity of criterion-referencing has arisen from different social and educational pressures through the 1970s, 1980s and 1990s. First, there is a strong consensus that the education system plays a crucial role in raising levels of skill and achievement in employment. This links to a view that employment and a licence to practise in different occupations should be based on clear, detailed descriptions of what people can actually do. There is a widespread view that the scant information about grades and rank orders that norm-referenced systems have traditionally provided is no longer adequate. Second, if more people are to be motivated to participate and achieve at higher levels, access to education and training should be based on more explicit and extensive definitions of what constitutes achievement and on clear criteria and standards to assess them. Third, if assessment is to motivate learners to achieve, these criteria should be at the heart of learning processes so that learners can take more control of their own education. These three aims are evident in the outcome-based or competence-based systems of NVQs and AVCEs, and in courses accredited by awarding bodies such as the Open College Network and the NCFE. Giving learners access to the public criteria by which their work is summatively assessed is now commonplace in A-levels, GCSEs and university degrees.

Criterion-referencing aims to remove the negative effects of rank-ordering learners by grades and comparing them with others. Instead, criterion-referenced assessment compares someone's performance with externally-defined, explicit criteria that aim to tell the assessor and the learner what level, range and type of performance is expected. It intends to:

- provide the basis for specific and detailed information about what someone can actually do and what they have achieved;
- describe the requirements for assessment and any grading which might take place so that they are more easily understood by learners, practitioners and assessors;
- provide a basis for objectively evaluating the curriculum and

the teaching and learning processes which underpin it;
- enable assessors and awarding bodies to verify judgements made about learners using the same publicly available criteria;
- make it easier for learners to seek accreditation of achievements gained outside formal learning programmes by relating them to explicit standards; and
- increase the accountability of learners, practitioners and institutions.

Criterion-referenced assessment is more likely to be used when:
- there is a desire to remove barriers in access to education, training and employment by being explicit about what entry requirements are; and
- access to a programme or licence to practise a craft or profession requires a clearer and more detailed description of competence than is provided through descriptions of rank order.

Ipsative (self-referenced) assessment

Ipsative assessment is an individualised form of criterion-referencing which measures a person's performance against self-defined criteria, derived from their previous performance. It can be used alongside other approaches since these criteria allow an individual learner to reach her or his own standard of achievement. In some programmes, however, it is sufficient on its own and other, externally-defined criteria need not be used. The process can build up confidence and the skills of self-assessment before learners move on to measurement against externally-defined standards.

However, ipsative assessment should not be associated only with confidence building or non-accredited programmmes. For many people certified as competent and skilled, ipsative assessment can be used in sophisticated ways to build evidence for licensing bodies, for putting a convincing job application together or simply updating a CV.

Ipsative assessment is more likely to be used when:
- learners want to chart their own progress and set their own targets;
- assessment against an external standard is not appropriate or required; or
- learners want or need to develop the ability to assess their own work independently of the tutor.

3. A framework for assessment

An assessment strategy

An organisational strategy for assessment enables practitioners and assessors to share their expertise with learners by being much more specific about the purposes and different levels of performance, and the criteria that underpin these. This clarity enables learners to be clearer and more confident about expectations. It also enables them to recognise what has been achieved and to set targets for improving performance. In addition, clarity leads to better descriptions of achievement and rank order to employers, admissions tutors and other external audiences.

Further benefits arise from analysing the learning outcomes that underpin different levels of achievement since this reduces the tendency to use implicit criteria that compare learners with each other, and provides more information on the strengths and weaknesses that produce different levels of performance. The effectiveness of assessment is increased if organisations use an assessment strategy to examine:

- implicit criteria which might be used by assessors, admissions tutors and employers;
- reasons for using particular forms of assessment at different stages of learning programmes;
- the various assessment activities offered across an institution;
- how assessment methods relate to learning outcomes and how evidence of these outcomes will be provided for a range of interested parties;
- how results will be recorded and interpreted by different users; and
- whether norm- and criterion-referenced and ipsative assessment are being used appropriately in learning programmes.

Different assessment activities

An assessment framework enables an education organisation to identify different assessment activities and to relate them to different purposes, the various people who might be involved and the resources that might be needed. These aspects of assessment are summarised in Figure 2 (pp 26–7).

The assessment framework discussed here enables practitioners and managers of assessment in institutions and awarding bodies to explore a number of aspects of assessment:

- different purposes of assessment at different stages of a learning programme, both for curriculum design and organisation and for inspection;
- assessment methods to suit different purposes;
- the range of skills that practitioners, tutors and learners need to make the most of assessment; and
- beliefs about assessment and traditions within different qualification systems held by both practitioners and learners.

Different assessment methods

The assessment framework can also inform staff development and training activities to help practitioners and assessors to:

- relate methods and techniques more clearly to the purpose of assessment;
- draw on a wider repertoire of methods;
- share good practice from different agencies and learning programme; and
- consider whether the methods they currently use are adapted appropriately to the purpose of assessment.

Tensions and areas of controversy

Discussions of purposes, types and methods of assessment show that it is important to be clear, both technically and conceptually, about how these aspects of assessment relate to each other. Yet such clarity is only partially useful. Strong political and social pressures pull the mindset and practices of practitioners and learners towards assessment that certificates achievement on behalf of external agencies. This mindset, and the pressure of targets, can lead to formative assessment being equated simplistically with a production line from diagnosis of needs to summative evidence of achievement based solely on the formal demands of a qualification. It is also common for many practitioners to equate formative assessment with continuous assessment. In a context of pressure to meet targets, this can become little more than the systematic accumulation of small summative assessments broken down from the demands of the qualification. This bears little relation to assessment that might be a genuine diagnosis of learning needs in order to build a learning programme with learners (see Chapter Three for further discussion).

In addition, many qualifications and learning programmes use a combination of ipsative, criterion-referenced and norm-referenced

Figure 2

Purpose of assessment	Learner wants/needs	Organisation provides or has access to
Initial Guidance ● to enable learner to make choices based on clear information about options and own abilities	● assessment for career direction ● assessment for aptitude ● design of a learning agreement or action plan ● review and assessment of prior learning *Assessment jointly by learner and someone in a guidance role (this may be a tutor or other professional, but could also be a peer, colleague or family member)*	● database of organisations and other local and national programmes or progression possibilities ● details of modules, assessment/accreditation/progression routes ● information about costs/ fees/grants ● taster courses or work experience placements that allow learners to diagnose their needs and existing abilities
Entry to Programme ● to provide information for teacher and managers of learning programmes ● to provide learner with a programme that meets needs, abilities and aspirations	● entry to learning programme (maybe without having traditional entry qualifications) ● decision about suitability for certification of prior learning for exemption from parts of the programme ● assessment of prior learning (e.g. through CV or application form) as basis for entry *Assessment is carried out by the person making an entry decision for the organisation*	● database of organisational programmes, modules, assessment, accreditation, progression opportunities ● official assessment and certification guidelines ● a range of skills tests or entry assignments ● clear outcomes and assessment criteria for all programmes offered by the organisation
In-Programme ● to provide information for practitioners and learners about progress, achievements and future needs ● to provide interim certification of modules or units leading to a full qualification	● review of progress ● recognition of achievement ● diagnosis of further needs/ learning targets ● opportunities to record achievements ● accumulation of grades/ competences *Assessment jointly by practitioners and learners*	● learning action plan ● tutorial support for review and ongoing guidance ● access to a bank of assignments and tests ● opportunities for work experience ● opportunities for review/ diagnosis with different teaching staff
Certification ● to provide information for employers, providers and admission tutors	● to be able to articulate what he or she has gained ● proof of attainment in the form of certificate/ record of achievement *Assessment is carried out by the person in the organisation who certificates achievement for the awarding body*	● employment and higher education application procedures ● admissions requirements in further and higher education ● flexible payment, registration and certification arrangements

People involved	Agencies or people carrying out the assessment	Techniques and methods

• careers officer/advisor
• guidance worker
• college/university central admissions
• college/university vocational/academic staff
• peers, friends and family
	• external careers and guidance services
	• the institution's central admissions office
	• staff from vocational/ academic programme areas
		• personal guidance interview
		• careers interest guides
		• self-assessment exercises
		• assessment of current competences
		• skills 'tasters'
		• work experience to diagnose aptitude and ability
		• initial diagnostic assessment
		• guidance interview:
		  – general
		  – subject specific
		• portfolio-building workshops

• tutor/teacher/trainer from specific programmes • admissions staff	• vocational/academic programmes • central admissions/ assessment unit • OCN tutors • AE tutors	• examination of references, application letters, portfolios • selection interview: – formal and informal • tests

• personal tutor
• vocational/academic assessors
• awarding body official
• careers officer/guidance worker
	• organisation where learning programme is taking place:
	  – individual staff
	  – college assessment unit
		• learning contracts or agreements
		• compiling in-course portfolios or records of achievement
		• assignments or projects
		• one-to-one/group/peer review
		• skills tests
		• diverse assessment exercises – oral, written, practical

• personal tutor • vocation/academic assessors • awarding body official	• vocational/academic staff • college central assessment unit	• summative record of achievement or final portfolio • final examinations/tests/ assignments

Figure 3 Assessment Methods

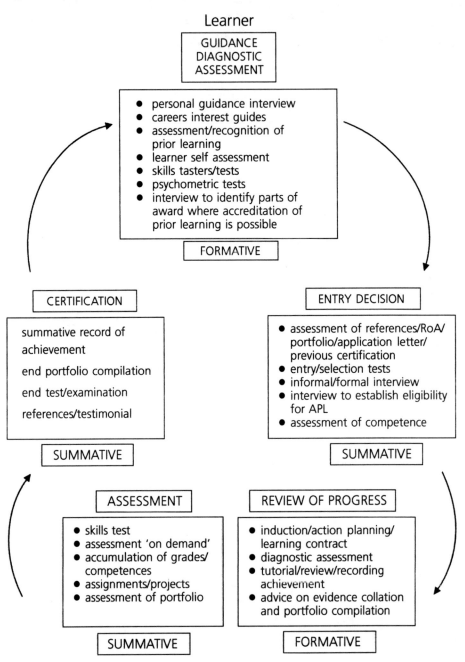

Learner

GUIDANCE DIAGNOSTIC ASSESSMENT

- personal guidance interview
- careers interest guides
- assessment/recognition of prior learning
- learner self assessment
- skills tasters/tests
- psychometric tests
- interview to identify parts of award where accreditation of prior learning is possible

FORMATIVE

CERTIFICATION

summative record of achievement

end portfolio compilation

end test/examination

references/testimonial

SUMMATIVE

ENTRY DECISION

- assessment of references/RoA/portfolio/application letter/previous certification
- entry/selection tests
- informal/formal interview
- interview to establish eligibility for APL
- assessment of competence

SUMMATIVE

ASSESSMENT

- skills test
- assessment 'on demand'
- accumulation of grades/competences
- assignments/projects
- assessment of portfolio

SUMMATIVE

REVIEW OF PROGRESS

- induction/action planning/learning contract
- diagnostic assessment
- tutorial/review/recording achievement
- advice on evidence collation and portfolio compilation

FORMATIVE

assessment but the reasons for using these forms of assessment are rarely made clear. Learners are often uncertain about what criteria are being used or how they relate to assessment methods or grading and marking systems. This can prevent learners from making the best use of their skills and previous experience. Although many accreditation systems are based on criterion-referenced assessment and disassociate themselves from norm-referencing, notions such as 'advanced', 'basic' and 'average' (and more negatively 'bright', 'able' and 'less-able') involve an implicit use of norms.

The summaries of norm- and criterion-referencing offered in this chapter make it important to note that the major qualification systems such as A-levels (vocational and general) and university degrees have moved a long way from traditional, 'hard' measures based on norm-referencing and standardisation of marks into a normal curve of distribution. Indeed, divisions between the two forms of referencing and the standards of achievement they imply are now extremely blurred (see Baird *et al*, 2000). For example, it is common to see outcome-based specifications and criteria of hierarchical grades that are derived from notions of 'excellent', 'good' and 'weak' levels of achievement, alongside non-graded statements of competence marked on a pass/fail basis.

It is also important to note that, despite attempts to make criterion-referenced or outcome-based assessment systems more transparent, there is a limit to how far words can ever express an absolute standard. In outcome-based qualifications, fundamental philosophical tension between what we know and can express, and what we know but cannot express in words, has dogged debates about the goals of 'transparency' and 'explicit' criteria. It has also led to a proliferation of words in the specifications, which have become more and more unwieldy. These problems show that any assessment criteria need ongoing discussion in order to help assessors, learners and other audiences interpret the criteria and the standards they imply; the specifications on their own are never sufficient (see Wolf, 1995; Winter and Maisch, 1996; Ecclestone, 2001 for detailed discussion of this problem).

A final discrepancy between the educationally progressive aims of criterion-referenced and outcome-based systems and actual practice arises from the way that teachers in any assessment system use a subconscious process of compensating, even when they are asked to apply the criteria strictly. Compensation takes account of the performance of a learner during an assessment task, the characteristics of the task (and whether teachers see them as fair or reasonable), and usual or expected performance of learners. Teachers make subconscious allowances, either liberally or strictly, depending on whether they judge the task to be difficult, complex or unfamiliar. Similarly, the 'halo effect' leads teachers to make other compensations if a normally competent learner performs in an uncharacteristically poor way. Or they might use other evidence of learners' abilities in unrelated attributes, such as confidence, diligence or good social skills, in interpreting criteria that do not require these attributes (see Wolf, 1995 and the account of GNVQ teachers in Ecclestone, 2002, for discussion of the subtle ways that compensation works).

There are, therefore, strong political, social and practical pressures on assessment practices, Discussion later in the book about the links between assessment and learning, and about the types of motivation and autonomy that an assessment system might foster, shows, however, that such pressures are also a result of viewing learning, knowledge and the building of knowledge and skills, in particular ways. These deeper philosophical tensions are discussed in future chapters, and some of their implications for assessment practices within institutions are discussed in Chapter Six.

References and further reading

Overview and analysis of the purposes and processes of assessment

Rowntree, D. (1987) *Assessing Students: how shall we know them?* London: Kogan Page.

Brown, S. and Knight, P. (1994) *Assessing Learners in Higher Education.* London: Kogan Page.

Discussion about the shift from norm to criterion-referencing in public examinations

Baird, J., Cresswell, M. and Newton, P. (2000) 'Would the real gold standard please step forward?' Research Papers in Education, 15, 2, 213–229.

Analysis of the need for induction and ongoing interpretation between assessors about the 'standards' of achievement implied by assessment criteria

Ecclestone, K. (2001) ' "I know a 2:1 when I see it": how lecturers learn degree standards in franchised programmes' in *Journal of Further and Higher Education*, 25, 3, 317–29.

Winter, R. and Maisch, R. (1996) *Professional Competence in Higher Education*. London: Falmer Press.
Wolf, A. (1995) *Competence-based Assessment*. Buckingham: Open University Press.

Discussion about the principles of using assessment to help learners to 'close the gap'

Gipps, C. (1994) *Beyond Testing: Towards a Theory of Educational Assessment*. London: Falmer Press.
Sadler, R. (1989) 'Formative assessment and the design of instructional systems' in *Instructional Science,* 18, 119–144.

Handbooks of assessment techniques and methods

Gibbs, G. (1986) *50 Ways to Make Your Assessment More Interesting*. Bristol: Technical Educational Services.
Race, P. and Brown, S. (1999: *500 Tips for Assessment*. London: Kogan Page.

CHAPTER 2

PRINCIPLES AND POLITICS IN ASSESSMENT AND CERTIFICATION

Introduction

The previous chapter argued for more technical and conceptual clarity about different purposes and types of assessment. It also highlighted some underlying political and social pressures on how qualification designers, external agenices, practitioners and learners regard these aspects of assessment. Despite these pressures, however, many agencies and organisations are trying to make the processes of assessment and accreditation more flexible. As the previous chapter showed, this reflects a general move to make education and training programmes more responsive to learners' needs by:

- making the content and organisation of learning programmes more flexible;
- being clearer about the requirements for a qualification by defining learning outcomes and linking them to assessment processes;
- promoting assessment methods that recognise achievement, support learning and help learners recognise what they can do, and the best way to apply their learning; and
- making progression routes clearer so that learners can plan their learning and move easily between agencies and programmes.

Aims for more participation and higher rates of achievement and progression are affected by social and cultural factors and expectations as well as by technical barriers to their realisation. On a purely technical level, achieving these aims is hindered by the confusing and complex array of qualifications and certificates that post-16 learners might take, offered by an equally bewildering array of bodies and agencies. In addition, the technical terms that describe different processes within qualifications and certificated programmes are often used interchangeably or in contradictory ways, between different formal systems.

In the light of this technical confusion, this chapter aims to:

- differentiate between key characteristics of assessment methods and link them to different purposes of assessment;
- relate characteristics to processes of evaluation in qualifications; and
- highlight how confusion produces conflicting ideas about standards in qualifications.

1. Key characteristics of assessment

In a similar way to debates about the relative emphasis that should be given to formative and summative assessment, debates about the relative value of reliability or validity in assessment systems can be traced back to wider questions about assessment's social functions. Different functions create tensions between selection and the desire for wider access, between the technical implications of a focus on a broad range of achievements and the narrower, more easily assessed achievements of paper-based examinations.

In part at least, the rise of outcome-based and criterion-referenced assessment systems reflects a desire to create assessment methods that might assess and recognise a broader range of real-life and employment-related achievements more accurately. Following discussion about the purposes and types of assessment in the last chapter, a method of assessment may have to demonstrate one or more of the following characteristics:

- reliability
- validity
- consistency
- authenticity
- dependability
- fairness

Reliability

In theory at least, reliable summative assessment enables institutions, awarding bodies and governments to generalise about the significance of results. Attempts to move away from hard, statistically-adjustable notions of reliability in the UK's old A- and O-level certificates and in university degrees, have led to softer versions of reliability in assessment, such as dependability, consistency and reproducibility. It is therefore possible to assume that when policy-makers, awarding body officials or practitioners themselves use these terms in relation to assessment, they are invoking, unwittingly or consciously, the notion of reliability.

In broad terms, then, a test or assessment that promotes reliability aims for:

- learners taking part in an assessment on one day to achieve broadly the same results at another time;
- markers or assessors agreeing on grades; and
- the quality of learners' work and assessors' interpretations of grades to be consistent.

Reliability is most easily gained when assessments can be standardised (for example, multiple choice tests or essays written under examination conditions) and when norms of performance in relation to written examinations or other assessments can be predicted and replicated. As discussion in Chapter One showed, reliability is integral to 'hard' systems of norm-referencing that use grading, rank-ordering and pre-determined percentages of achievement across a normal curve of distribution for the purposes of selection.

Reliability is more likely to be achieved when:

- learners taking the assessment have similar abilities and aptitudes;
- assessment has to differentiate between the best and worst performances that might be expected from a 'typical' cohort; and
- assessors have to agree and be consistent in their interpretations of the relative performance of a cohort's work.

When reliability is used to underpin assessment for selection, awarding bodies and test designers might use statistical measurements of results, together with processes such as moderating assessors' grading decisions to ensure a spread of marks (see Chapter Four for discussion of moderation). In broader terms, processes and techniques to maximise reliability in summative assessment include:

- a focus on measuring one underlying attribute or knowledge in a particular test item, based on the predicted norms of the cohort being tested (past examination papers and 'typical' learners' answers are an important basis for judging this);
- procedures to standardise and statistically measure learners' responses;
- processes to maximise the likelihood of consistency in assessors' interpretations; for example, analytical marking schemes require

assessors to award a specific number of marks for specific, pre-defined features in learners' work;
- procedures to average grades over several examination papers marked by different assessors; and
- rules to prevent assessors being involved with their own learners' summative performance (hence the use in some qualifications of a team of subject markers employed by examination boards).

Some problems with tests designed to maximise reliability are that:
- they can be too narrow and not indicate a true reflection of learners' capabilities;
- learners may not see the tests as valid and authentic and might therefore 'jump through hoops' instrumentally in order to pass the test with minimum effort;
- they require a relatively small number of well-qualified assessors who can discuss their interpretation of criteria and norms of achievement;
- they require moderation and sampling to ensure fairness, especially when selection for employment or higher education is competitive;
- they are not good at predicting learners' future performance; and
- the need to standardise tests for reliability detracts from their real-life relevance: for example, the same rehearsed role-play gives the same performance to ensure similar test conditions, but is very artificial and therefore lacks validity as a reflection of authentic performance (West, 2000).

Validity

Valid assessment enables different interested groups and stakeholders in education and training to interpret learners' performance in settings and contexts that are as authentic as possible. Valid assessment should predict that someone's competence or performance is sound and will continue to be so. Valid methods should therefore measure the skills or attributes they claim to measure. This goal produces the well-known claim invoked by supporters of competence-based assessment, namely that it is invalid to assess someone's ability to drive a car (for example) by using a written examination.

Valid assessment aims for test designers and assessors to:
- infer that learners will be able to apply the skill or attribute being tested in the formal assessment situation in future situations;

- present meaningful descriptions of the purpose, scope and methods of assessment that relate to the learning outcomes specified for summative assessment;
- use 'real-life', authentic methods to assess different skills, knowledge and attributes; and
- define the types of evidence and criteria for performance that will comprise a valid assessment.

The goal of validity in a qualification or assessment model was a strong feature of assessment policy and practice during the 1980s and 1990s. Combined with moves towards criterion-referenced assessment, the goal of validity has eroded hard measures of reliability through norm-referencing. It has also led to an emphasis in quality assurance and awarding body procedures on:

- clarifying expectations about standards and assessment criteria and the quality and quantity of evidence expected from learners;
- establishing processes to moderate assessors' judgements in order to maximise validity rather than reliability; and
- developing exemplars of 'typical' work for indicating the expected quality and standards that learners should achieve.

Validity is more likely to be important for:

- assessing work place skills (for example, for promotion or recruitment) and granting a licence to practise a profession; and
- building up a picture of someone's ability and attributes over time, such as through a record of achievement or other forms of portfolio systems that might include artefacts, testimonials and other evidence of achievement.

Problems with assessment activities designed for validity are:

- the cost of authenticity (for example, finding sufficient time for assessment in real-life situations with real-life assessors from authentic settings);
- finding enough realistic opportunities to be assessed in 'real life'; for example, many jobs do not offer a range of opportunities for learners to show their competence;
- ensuring a consistency of interpretations of the criteria amongst a diverse range of assessors;
- finding the time and resources to enable different assessors to discuss their interpretations of the criteria; this has tended to produce endless attempts to specify the criteria in more detail and

to issue more written 'guidance' in place of face-to-face meetings; and
- the difficulty of using the results of assessments designed for validity for the purposes of comparing centres in order to evaluate national standards of achievement (see below in Section 3).

As this section makes clear, the notion of *authenticity* is related closely to validity: authentic assessment has credibility with practitioners, learners and the end-users of qualifications because it is realistic and reflects closely the skill or attribute it is designed to recognise formally. Authentic assessment also indicates that it takes place in real-life contexts rather than artificial conditions.

Fairness
It is clear from the definitions above that reliability and validity imply different things for the design and purpose of assessment. Yet while it is possible to have assessments that prioritise reliability at the expense of validity, and vice versa, most assessment systems try to achieve both features.

Nevertheless, each feature has different implications for how we regard fairness in assessment. In a highly selective system, for example, candidates for assessment need to be assured that steps are taken to maximise reliability: anonymity, blind marking and tests taken at the same time all offer a particular notion of 'fairness'. If, on the other hand, someone is being selected on the basis of a test to do a particular job, 'fairness' derives from maximising authenticity in the assessment. In this case, valid assessments, such as a portfolio of evidence, testimonials, skills tests and observation, would carry a different notion of 'fairness' from that in reliable tests (see West, 2000 for discussion).

2. Evaluation and quality assurance

Evaluation is crucial to decision-making amongst practitioners and within organisations about the quality of provision, teaching and learning. It involves making judgements about the worth of an activity, based on the systematic, open collection and analysis of data. The outcomes of summative assessment are a crucial, yet only partial, source of this data. Other sources, such as student and staff surveys and inspection data, are also important. The focus of evaluation should relate to explicit objectives, criteria and values.

Unsurprisingly perhaps, evaluation in post-16 organisations is now steered by the demands of external inspection, perhaps to the exclusion of different values regarding evaluation. This makes it important to reassert the importance of evaluation carried out by practitioners rather than by institutional managers or external bodies and inspectors.

In contrast, a teacher-centred notion of evaluation diagnoses a learning experience already in use by learners and questions its effects. In teaching, evaluation requires collection and analysis of information about the results of learners' encounters with a learning or assessment experience. Ideally, evaluation of this kind might enable teachers to understand what it is like to learn within the system they have created and to identify which objectives have been achieved. Formal assessments, informal observation and discussion with colleagues and learners all enable teachers to create similar or better learning experiences for other learners.

It is, however, important to recognise the extent to which 'assessment' and 'evaluation' are used loosely and inter changeably in the everyday language of teaching and inspection. One solution is to confine the term 'assessment' to activities associated with making judgments about learning and achievement, as described and delineated in Chapter One, and to use 'evaluation' for judgments associated with the quality of provision and systems for organising learning and assessment. This distinction is not robust in semantic terms but it does help to clarify these diverse activities in a complex education and training system.

Different types of evaluation

Evaluation can be internal and external, formative and summative. As with assessment of learners, different methods and data for evaluation can serve different purposes and audiences. It is therefore helpful to differentiate explicitly and as precisely as possible which data is needed for which purposes and who should collect and use the data. The broad difference between formative and summative purposes of evaluation is that formative outcomes are not made public and practitioners are not held accountable. Instead, formative evaluation emphasises developmental processes rather than measurable public outcomes.

It is crucial to differentiate between formative and summative purposes because it helps clarify more precisely which audiences and stakeholders have a legitimate interest in the processes and outcomes of evaluation.

Formative evaluation

This form of evaluation:

- looks critically at the kinds of educational goals being set, their function within curriculum development and their implications for staff development; and
- considers the extent to which the goals of summative evaluation are being met *before* the summative (formal, official) evaluation takes place.

Summative evaluation

This form of evaluation:

- focuses on meeting demands for accountability towards pre-defined goals and criteria;
- involves judgements about the extent to which these goals have been achieved and whether sanctions or rewards should be applied (for example, funding allocations tied to meeting targets);
- is carried out for external bodies, especially government bodies, and is therefore both public and official;
- aims for system-wide comparison of quality against national criteria (this focuses evaluation on measures of 'reliability'); and
- is used in the UK as a lever for curriculum change.

Following a differentiation between formative and summative purposes, evaluation can be:

- external and formative (carried out with help and support from external or internal advisers and as part of staff and curriculum development);
- external and summative (carried out by inspectors);
- internal and formative (carried out by individual practitioners about their own or colleagues' practice in teaching and assessment, perhaps in learning groups or 'quality circles'); or
- internal and summative, (carried out by peers and managers as part of preparation for inspection or for formal institutional 'self-assessment'. (This term reflects the inspectorates' confusing use of 'assessment' to mean 'evaluation'!))

Evaluations can therefore be both internal and external, and aim to meet diagnostic, formative and summative purposes. In similar ways to confusion about the purposes of assessment, lack of clarity can create problems for practitioners and institutional managers.

Quality assurance

In qualifications and assessment, it is helpful to regard quality assurance as comprising processes that aim to reduce sources of error in assessment caused by particular, local circumstances whilst preserving the overall validity of assessment. Broadly, quality assurance processes develop agreement about quality and monitors progress. However, a study of quality assurance and quality control in post-16 qualifications shows that awarding bodies, the QCA and inspectors all use the terms 'quality assurance' and 'quality control' interchangeably (Ecclestone and Hall, 1998). Despite confusion in day-to-day practices, it might be helpful to try to differentiate more clearly between the two terms.

Processes for quality assurance might include:

- approving centres to run tests and curricula against centrally-designed and evaluated criteria (also known as validation);
- developing exemplar materials of tests and learning materials;
- developing guidance for centres to follow;
- carrying out internal moderation of assessment results (standardising the outcomes of assessment in relation to validity and reliability); and
- carrying out internal verification of assessment results (checking that procedures have been followed).

Internal verifiers and moderators might work across different programme and level types within an organisation. However, ethos and tone in such processes are important, especially with peers and colleagues, since merely checking, remarking and adjusting marks without genuine dialogue or negotiation is unlikely to produce a professional commitment to improving assessment (please see Chapter Four for further discussion of moderation and verification).

Quality control

In qualifications and assessment, it might be helpful to regard quality control as comprising processes that aim to ensure public accountability for the results or outcomes of summative assessments carried out in local contexts. These processes might be both internal and external, but their emphasis is summative rather than formative. They might include:

- moderating assessors' judgements and decisions (for example, external moderators acting on behalf of an awarding body); regional and national moderation meetings with practitioners and evaluators; postal sampling; in-house sampling of assessment results by internal or external evaluators;

- verifying that quality assurance and control procedures have been adhered to within centres and by assessors acting on behalf of centres; and
- offering national quality awards for best practice in quality assurance and quality control.

The blurring of formative and summative evaluation, and of quality assurance and quality control, has led to dilemmas among external moderators and verifiers about how far to treat such processes as developmental and supportive and how far they should adopt a more remote, summative approach as the official representatives of awarding bodies. A blurring of roles has led some awarding bodies to adopt more distant, impersonal quality control procedures, such as postal sampling and moderation of learners' assignments, rather than face-to-face visits.

3. Tensions and areas of controversy

Although old systems of hard norm-referencing and methods to maximise reliability in qualifications have declined, reliability is still a central goal of quality assurance procedures used by awarding bodies and the Qualifications and Curriculum Authority (QCA). More recently, this goal has been in conflict with validity as a key feature of outcome-based systems in National Vocational Qualifications (NVQs) and GNVQs. In these qualifications, designers wanted policy-makers, awarding bodies, inspectors and end-users of qualifications, such as employers and higher education institutions, to accept a high premium on validity and place less emphasis on reliability, its supporters arguing that this shift would maximise the credibility of qualifications. In addition, precise specification of criteria and standards for assessment would help to ensure consistency between assessors on what counted as valid performance. In theory, then, better validity would lead to reliability. The debate about 'standards', summarised below, shows how technically and politically contentious this attempt to move qualifications towards validity has been.

There is therefore much debate amongst qualification designers and policy-makers about the meanings of features such as reliability and validity, as well as about their respective desirability in different qualifications. On a simple technical level, confusion about features of assessment and evaluation affects everyday understanding and practice. Nevertheless, it is possible to be clearer about each characteristic and to promote better understanding about the goals and activities of different assessment systems, between learners, practitioners, inspectors and awarding body officials and external agencies.

Developments in qualification systems over the past twenty years reveal deeper political and social uncertainty about how characteristics such as reliability and validity, norm-referencing and criterion-referencing should be applied in different assessment systems in order to meet different social needs (see discussion in Raggatt and Williams, 1999; West, 2000). Such confusion is exacerbated by lack of a clear public debate about the characteristics that assessment systems should have in order to meet different purposes.

Nowhere is tension about the purposes of assessment and its characteristics more apparent than in the annual furore over standards in education. Each summer, the publication of A-level and GCSE results produces a fraught, contradictory debate in the media about whether standards in the English education system are rising or falling. Tensions in the system, and in public, political and professional attitudes to assessment came to a head in the summer of 2002. The fallout from problems with A-level grading both reflected, and arose from, fundamental questions about the purposes of qualifications and the types of assessment they should use. It is interesting to use the experience of 2002 to reflect on these questions and their impact on ideas about assessment.

Eighteen-year-olds born in the post-war boom year of 1947 took their A-levels in 1965. They were unlikely to be aware of the extent to which examining bodies had to adjust grade boundaries that year in order to maintain a fixed number of A-grades. A-levels were therefore much 'harder' than in previous years but the same percentage were 'good enough' to go on to university. The rest accepted their fate. In 1974, for example, only eight per cent of the cohort was told they were good enough to go into higher education because they were the most intelligent of their age group. This misplaced sense of superiority offered images of fairness that enabled students to accept the effects of divisive grading in A-levels. Crucially, this depended on not knowing how the grading was done but also on the idea that the examination tested intelligence and that not everyone was intelligent enough to get the best grades. Past acceptance of 'hard norm-referencing' (or 'cohort-referencing') in Advanced levels (A-levels) and the Ordinary Certificate of General Education (O-levels) until 1988 was therefore underpinned by ideas that intelligence could be measured.

It can be argued that such ideas have been eroded, but not removed, by a shift towards what Baird *et al* call 'weak criterion-referencing', which began with the change from O-levels to General Secondary Certificates in Education (GCSE) in 1988.

The depth of public and professional indignation about a last-ditch attempt by the Oxford, Cambridge and RSA awarding body (OCR) to stave off a very high pass rate in A-level results for 2002 is a stark contrast to previous acceptance of rank ordering and selection through qualifications. The A-level grading problems of 2002 reflect profound political and professional problems about how to create trust in the ability of policy and qualification bodies to manage 'standards' in the education system as a whole. In turn, confusion about standards and their regulation creates challenges for assessment experts trying to explain to diverse audiences what has happened and why.

Press coverage of A-levels in 2002 used the language of 'slash and burn', 'fixing of grades', 'scandal', 'fiasco' and 'crude and brutal fixing'. In contrast to older ideas of fairness based on selective grading and rank-ordering, this populist debate focused on the unjustness of the process for young people who had worked so hard and should have 'got the grades they deserved'. In order to deflect growing calls for her resignation, the Secretary of State for Education, Estelle Morris, highlighted the need to 'sort the problem out for the sake of our young people's futures'.

Despite such expressions of concern, an unprecedented tone of mistrust and blame emerged between parents, pupils and the awarding bodies, the QCA and awarding bodies; between awarding bodies and their own subject examiners; and between the QCA and politicians. Mistrust and allegations of incompetence in the awarding bodies accompanied disagreement between the three unitary awarding bodies about how they should have dealt with predictions of the very high pass rates that emerged during the marking of A-level scripts in June and July 2002.

The QCA's own four-day inquiry did not stave off concerns. Indeed, it fuelled them by concluding that there was no fixing and that, instead, teachers had misunderstood the standard of coursework that was required in the new assessment regime for A-levels. A public investigation, led by the ex-chief inspector of schools, Mike Tomlinson, was supposed to reveal whether political interference by the Secretary of State and head of the QCA had led to harsh adjustments of the grade boundaries that are always agreed with examiners at the beginning of the marking process.

Arguably, this investigation fudged the deeper tensions between norm- and criterion-referenced assessment by presenting the grading problems as a technical accident waiting to happen, brought about by an over-hasty introduction of new first- and second-year assessment regimes in A-levels. The 2,000 scripts sent for re-grading after the investigation was the same number as the normal number re-marked after appeals in any year. In addition to token re-grading, the ex-chief inspector of schools also called for "clear definitions of the toughness of the qualification".

Media coverage revealed old beliefs in psychometric measures of ability, implicit in labels such as 'bright', 'less able' or 'weak' students were still largely accepted, and conjecture that a once-objective examination system to measure ability had become dishonest. For example, a confusing editorial in the Daily Telegraph argues that the refusal of the head of OCR to resign shows that "such insouciance on the part of those in authority is almost more shocking than the scandal itself". After berating the authorities for 'cheating' students of their deserved grades, it shifts, erratically, to concerns that 'more means worse':

> "The Government's aim is to accustom the country to a system
> that is no longer designed, as the A-level originally was, to
> identify the academic minority who will benefit from a good
> university but is intended, rather, to equip pupils of average
> ability with a qualification that will enable them to enter higher
> education and find a job." (*Daily Telegraph*, 2002)

The A-level grading problem of 2002, and the media coverage that accompanied it, highlighted the extent to which problems in a high-stakes examination system continue to be obfuscated, albeit mainly unwittingly.

Interestingly, the same debates do not appear with the same political and media force in Scotland, Ireland or Wales, nor in the vocational training system. Indeed, the results of vocational education courses are rarely discussed in the media. Nor does discussion about national standards appear in other European countries. In contrast, political, popular and professional debates in England reflect confusion and disagreement about what 'standards of achievement' and 'fairness in education' mean. This sensitivity has led to recent attempts to generate agreement on parity of esteem between very diverse qualifications in the national framework by focusing on external assessment, regardless of the type of qualification and learners taking it.

Although debates about standards in qualifications are complicated, it is possible to discern two broad positions:
- standards are best measured through norm-referenced assessment that enables judgements to be made about consistent, but selective,

achievement based on reliable assessment decisions and comparisons about standards of achievement over time; and
- high standards measure attainment based on valid, authentic decisions and more detailed accounts of achievement.

Each interpretation offers a different meaning of what constitutes 'fair' assessment. Policy-makers and qualification designers must balance both meanings, together with the technical assessment and quality assurance mechanisms that promote them. This task is fraught, complex and little-understood by those undertaking it (see, for example, West, 2000) Tensions reflect different purposes for qualifications where, in broad terms, reliability meets a need for fair treatment of candidates in high stakes or selective assessment and validity fulfils a requirement to confirm publicly that someone is competent or licensed to practice. One effect of combining these purposes within qualifications is that the technical issues surrounding debates about 'standards' are already complex, even before political considerations are added to them.

Political debates around standards illustrate deep-rooted ideological and social disagreements about which types of assessment and knowledge should have higher social status (see Young, 1998). The resulting fault-line runs through the qualification system, producing assessment policy that simultaneously sets tougher targets to motivate more people to achieve formal qualifications, while at the same time fuelling concern that more achievement must mean lower standards (see Stanton, 1998; Ecclestone, 2002 for discussion about these debates in policy-making for vocational and general qualification).

It is interesting to consider how problems with different meanings of 'standards' in assessment and qualifications reflect the ways in which certain words embody practices and institutions embedded within culture and society at any given time. Problems over meanings are therefore inextricably bound up with the problem the word is being used to discuss in a particular historical and political context. Raymond Williams analyses in detail the word 'standards' as "an exceptional kind of plural...a plural singular" (Williams, 1983, p. 296), where disagreeing with one meaning implies, in the case of 'standards', disagreeing with the idea of quality itself. Since very different values underpin 'standards' in assessment policy, it is not insignificant that 'morals' and 'values' are the other two examples Williams gives of plural singulars.

According to Williams, the historical evolution of a standard shows its symbolic status as a flag or banner behind which warring sides would rally. The idea of a banner, or standard, aligns with the moral status of 'standards' as a quality of performance or behaviour that must both be defended and maintained. The blurring of 'standard' as both a rallying call and a moral appeal to maintain standards is therefore very evident in assessment policy, particularly in England.

Other meanings of 'standards' are also powerful and create further confusion. The notion of standardising a product to a particular level of quality is represented, as Williams argues, in the British Standard or the flower known as the 'standard rose'. This image underpins both the exhaustive specifications of occupational standards in NVQs and approaches taken in some qualifications to making sure that practitioners interpret criteria consistently. A quality assurance vision of standards, based on strict protocols for assessment and moderation processes, is exemplified in the bureaucratic approach adopted in the QCA's Code of Practice for awarding bodies.

Each of the meanings of 'standards' discussed above is used implicitly or overtly to attack or defend a particular stance in assessment policy (see the accounts of Advanced GNVQ policy-making in Ecclestone, 2002; Ecclestone, 2000). At the same time, each notion also underpins a sophisticated technological armoury of testing, monitoring and moderation methods. These are enormously complicated for practitioners and awarding body officials to understand and use effectively. The overall effect is to make any discussion about standards both complex and fraught.

It seems that when qualifications are required to fulfil competing purposes in the national framework, bids for parity of esteem seem to drift towards demands for more reliability: hence the current emphasis in growing numbers of qualifications on external tests. This is reinforced by mechanisms that awarding bodies adopt for quality assurance and control to gain reliable and consistent interpretations of criteria between practitioners. Such an emphasis makes it difficult for qualifications that may not need to show reliability in learners' achievement but which may aim to promote ideas about valid and authentic assessment.

Nevertheless, confusion suggests that some clarity about principles and processes, together with some recognition of political pressures, might help practitioners and learners to make day-to-day assessment and evaluation processes more meaningful.

References and further reading

Discussion about the complexities and implications of meanings about 'standards' in assessment policy
Baird, J., Cresswell, M. and Newton, P. (2000) 'Would the real gold standard please step forward?' *Research Papers in Education*, 15, 2, 213–229.

Discussion of validity and reliability in outcome-based assessment systems
Jessup, G. (1991) *Outcomes: NVQs and the emerging model of education and training*. London: Falmer Press.
Wolf, A. (1995) *Competence-based Assessment*. Buckingham: Open University Press.

Discussion of validity and reliability in assessment
West, J. (2000) *Validity and Reliability in Qualifications: technical and political considerations*. Unpublished MA Dissertation. Sheffield: University of Sheffield.
Wilmut, J. (1999) *Internal Assessment*. London: Qualifications and Curriculum Authority.

Analyses of post-16 assessment and qualifications policy
Ecclestone, K. (2000) 'Bewitched, bothered and bewildered: a policy analysis of the GNVQ assessment regime' in *Journal of Education Policy*, 15, 3, 539–558
Ecclestone, K. (2002) *Learning Autonomy in Post-16 Education: the policy and practice of formative assessment*. London: Routledge/Falmer Press.
Raggatt, P. and Williams, S. (1999) *Government, Markets and Qualifications*. London: Falmer Press.
Stanton, G. (1998) 'Patterns in Development', in Tomlinson, S. (ed.) (1998) *Education 14-19: Critical Perspectives*. London: Athlone Press.

Discussion of 'standards'
Goldstein, H. and Heath, A. (eds) (2000) *Educational Standards*. Oxford: Oxford University Press/British Academy.

Williams, R. (1983) *Keywords: A Vocabulary of Culture and Society.* London: Fontana Press.

Discussion of the social and cultural role of qualifications and different types of curricula

Young, M. (1998) *The Curriculum of the Future.* London: Falmer Press.

CHAPTER 3

USING ASSESSMENT TO ENHANCE LEARNING

Introduction

While it is helpful to regard diagnostic assessment as a sub-category of formative assessment, many practitioners and institutional managers associate it increasingly with initial assessment or screening, for example for literacy and numeracy skills. This association with formal tests is encouraged by the way that funding and targets for retention give diagnostic testing a semi-summative role. Some schools and colleges use literacy and numeracy tests for screening before they make a summative assessment decision to offer a place on a particular course (see Chapter One).

It is therefore possible to use a formal diagnostic test or other assessment, such as a well-designed learning style inventory, as a basis for teaching and learning activities and to determine appropriate formative feedback. Such an assessment might also be used as an immediate precursor to a summative decision about entry to a particular programme, so its outcomes might be communicated to tutors at the next stage.

An increasing number of institutions also use 'value-added' assessments of existing grades or levels of achievement to predict expected grades, or to compare the differences between characteristics of learners at the beginning of a programme and at the end. Pressures for retention and achievement targets often link initial screening and diagnostic assessment directly with the right kinds of support during a learning programme. In some colleges, students are allocated 'learning managers', ostensibly to support those who might not be seen to be achieving in line with their predicted grades during ongoing summative assessments. Whilst potentially progressive, these measures might increase a tendency for institutions to recruit those learners who are likely to stay the course and to achieve at the end, or to encourage learners to meet criteria instrumentally, without much engagement with learning.

At the same time, the transition from formative to summative assessment is increasingly blurred, particularly in programmes where summative results accumulate from coursework and assignments. This leads to the widespread belief that formative assessment is synonymous with 'continuous assessment' or courses without end examinations.

These conflicting purposes make diagnostic and formative assessment confusing. Different purposes, and different stages where diagnostic assessment might be used, also mean that decisions about how to use the outcomes are as much strategic and resource-based as they are educational.

This chapter aims to:

- identify different stages for diagnostic assessment with a learning programme;
- examine the links between assessment and learning;
- highlight some barriers to effective diagnosis and formative feedback; and
- identify strategies for improving diagnostic and formative assessment within institutions.

1. Different stages of diagnostic assessment

Pre-programme guidance

Initial guidance is a diagnostic process that offers new learners, or those already familiar with the institution but who are progressing to a new stage, a chance to assess their past achievements and decide on support and areas of work they need to attend to. The main purpose of diagnosis for these learners is therefore *formative*: it offers a basis for future support and for making a decision about the best option to follow.

Activities at this stage could include:

- general advice and counselling;
- discussions about CVs, or other records of achievement;
- formal testing of skills and attributes.

Although the audience for this formative assessment is primarily the learner, it is important to clarify whether other tutors and teachers will need the information for subsequent stages of the learning programme. A strategic approach to initial guidance therefore requires organisations to decide:

- which groups or types of learners will need informal or formal diagnostic assessment before a programme begins;

- what skills will be the focus of diagnoses and what methods or approach will be used; and
- which staff or other audience will need information about the outcomes of diagnoses (such as learning support units, study skills tutors, personal tutors etc.).

At the beginning of modules or programmes of study

Formal and *informal* diagnostic assessment activities might therefore include:

- specific assessments of aptitudes or skills;
- ability testing at the beginning of a programme that might be compared statistically with those at the end ('value-added' measures);
- assignments that enable learners to make initial attempts at reaching the required standard of work, with formative feedback, before a formal, summative assignment.

In everyday teaching and tutoring activities, the notion of 'diagnosis' enables teachers (and students themselves) to monitor students' responses and the difficulties they might be having. Once diagnostic assessment is seen in this formative, learning-related way, activities such as classroom and tutorial questioning and marking students' course work or assignments, enable teachers to diagnose strengths, gaps and problems and to offer formative advice for future work.

2. Assessment as part of learning

Diagnostic assessment

Processes and activities to find out the difficulties that groups or individual learners have in meeting the demands of a course are integral to everyday classroom or workplace activities, questions and coursework. While most teachers and tutors tend not to regard these activities and interactions either as diagnostic or as an assessment, thinking about the notion of diagnostic assessment helps to make these intuitive or unconscious activities more strategic. Black and Wiliam point to the links between diagnostic and formative assessment as part of everyday teaching:

> *"Essential elements of any strategy to improve learning through implementation of formative assessment . . . would be the setting of clear goals, the choice, framing and articulation of*

appropriate learning tasks, the deployment of these with
appropriate pedagogy to evoke feedback . . . and the appropriate
interpretation and use of that feedback to guide the learning
trajectory of students." (1998, p. 61)

The importance of involving learners through self and peer assessment is also clear and Black and Wiliam frame their discussion of formative assessment within a constructivist approach to learning. This approach is discussed in more depth in Chapter Five.

In similar ways to the outcomes of diagnostic assessment at the stage of initial guidance, institutions need to decide who needs information about the outcomes of diagnostic assessment at the beginning of, or during, a learning programme. In addition, course teams or individual tutors are likely to have their own good practices that can form the basis for a more strategic approach across the institution.

Informal diagnostic activities include:

- teachers' everyday observations of responses to questions and activities;
- feedback by teachers on whether responses to questions etc. relate to the required standard of work;
- learners' self assessment of work before and after submission for feedback, using the assessment criteria; and
- learners' peer assessment of each other's work.

Formative assessment

Despite growing interest in formative assessment, shown by bodies such as the QCA, it appears to be widely misunderstood. It is either too narrowly conceptualised as feedback on students' work, or target-setting in relation to summative criteria, or too broadly conceptualised as pedagogy to encourage reflection amongst learners about their learning. Black and Wiliam (1998) offer a broad definition that enables teachers and learners to regard particular principles and methods as integral to formative assessment:

"Formative assessment is a moment of learning and students
have to be active in their own assessment and to picture their
own learning in the light of an understanding of what it means
to get better." (ibid, p. 29)

Principles of effective diagnostic and formative assessment

There is a growing body of research about how children, young people and adults regard processes of assessment and feedback. This research points to positive strategies for improving processes of diagnosis, target-setting and feedback, and some of these are summarised here. However, it also shows that there are complex social and cultural processes embedded within assessment activities that have a powerful impact on the shaping of learning identities. This section refers briefly to these factors but cannot do justice to the complexity of subtle issues of power between teachers and learners, the importance of learners' self-identity, and the social dynamics embedded within everyday assessment activities. (For further discussion, see Pollard and Filer, 1999; Reay and William, 1999; Ecclestone and Pryor, 2003; James, 2000.)

Research on formal and informal assessment activities designed with diagnosis and formative feedback in mind highlights some underpinning principles:

- diagnostic assessment should focus on a person's *potential* ability not fixed traits of intelligence or personality;
- learners need their own diagnostic skills if they are to become independent from teachers and able to judge their own work in relation to the criteria;
- the notion of 'internalising the criteria' emerges through knowing what constitutes a high-quality piece of work and what a poor one;
- the notion of 'closing the gap' between where learners are and the quality of work they are aiming for is crucial to internalising the criteria and diagnosing strengths, weaknesses and next steps;
- 'closing the gap' requires much more engagement than merely ensuring that learners are meeting the requirements by going through a set of procedures;
- information that teachers gain from diagnosis does not become feedback until it makes a difference to learners' performances;
- learners have to engage proactively with feedback in order to incorporate it into an internalised, personally authentic under-standing of what it means to improve ;
- feedback is neither diagnostic or formative unless learners can *act* upon it: without action or engagement, feedback remains a summative statement of achievement or of weaknesses.

(For further discussion see Gipps, 1995; Black and Wiliam, 1998, 2005; Ecclestone, 2002; Black 2005.)

3. Barriers to effective diagnosis and formative feedback

If formative and diagnostic assessment are seen as integral to teaching and learning, it becomes easier for teachers and learners to decide which classroom and assessment activities might form a basis for diagnosing barriers to learning and where feedback needs to help learners do better next time. It also helps them to recognise where assessments that might appear to be formative are more precisely part of ongoing, or continuous summative, assessments. This distinction is important because many teachers regard coursework assignments as formative simply if they come before a final assessment. Another misconception is that formative assessment is 'practice' assessment. As section two argued, much coursework is actually summative in purpose and audience.

Identifying the principles behind effective diagnosis and feedback also enables teachers to make a similarly strategic review of their current assessment and feedback activities. This involves identifying some barriers to a productive communication about the criteria with learners, and helping learners to close the gap between their current and potential achievement. Such barriers include:

Technical difficulties:
- written and oral feedback and advice about strengths and weaknesses in students' work may be confusing, opaque or vague, making it difficult for them to know how to use or act upon it;
- feedback and advice from individual teachers, or across teams, may cover the same range of general points in each assignment so that learners either believe they have too many points to address in future work, or that the points are too big to address;
- learners might see feedback and advice given alongside or just after a summative grade as negative or positive confirmations of an existing learning identity (ie. 'yet another fail, another distinction') and so do not see a need to act upon it.

Professional roles:
- notions of what 'meeting the standards' really involves are often tacit and learned by teachers in informal, *ad hoc* ways through marking, informal moderation of each others' marking and discussions with awarding body officials;

- profound pressures on teachers and students to meet summative targets can render formative feedback as little more than instrumental advice on how to add bits of extra information to meet the criteria;
- many teachers do not take part in development activities to reflect on and improve feedback strategies and techniques.

Learners' misunderstandings:
- learners often regard advice that teachers intend to be formative as additional summative confirmation of achievement or short-comings, leading them to reject it;
- many learners see any classroom questioning as public, summative tests of knowledge and understanding, and are therefore more or less confident, depending on past experience or ideas about their own ability;
- individual learners may respond very differently to the tone and phrasing of formative feedback at the beginning of a learning programme than they might do at the end;
  learners may not see self and peer assessment as legitimate processes because assessment is something 'done to them' by teachers (ie. they see it as the teacher's job alone, rather than theirs);
- previous experiences of assessment have profound effects on learners' understanding of new systems they take part in.

4. Strategies for improving formative and diagnostic assessment

Discussion in this chapter, and in Chapter One, suggests that teachers and institutions need to be clearer and more explicit about the different purposes and timings of assessment activities and to explain and discuss them with learners. More clarity would also mean that teachers spend less time on writing or giving feedback that learners find difficult to use or act upon, and more time on targeted or strategic feedback, and on types of classroom and individual questioning that help learners to review progress and diagnose barriers to learning. Critically, broader concepts of diagnosis and formative feedback enable important classroom and training activities and everyday interactions to be used for diagnostic and formative purposes.

It is also perhaps important to note here that teachers need to differentiate clearly between summative or formative purposes of self and peer assessment and recording of achievement so that students are clear about the audience and purpose of a judgement on someone else's work or on their own work.

Strategies for making formative and diagnostic assessment more effective include:

Activities with learners:

- discussing the different purposes and timing of assessment activities;
- discussing different ideas about learning that underpin assessment systems (see Chapter Four);
- separating confirmation of a summative grade from diagnostic and formative advice and explaining to students why it is important to give feedback *before* the formal grade;
- requiring learners to self-assess their work, or that of their peers, before receiving a summative grade;
- using the types of moderation activities usually carried out with colleagues in order to help students compare different qualities and standards of work.

Activities with colleagues:

- planning which assignments will focus on particular areas of knowledge and skill and confining feedback on how to improve work in those areas;
- developing a portfolio of exemplar assignments or objects based on past students' work (anonymised for the purpose) and using these in practice marking activities with students;
- being clear about whether self and peer assessment activities have formative or summative purposes and outcomes, and whether it is appropriate for these types of assessment to be used for summative purposes;
- considering how the classroom climate and relationships between peers will affect self and peer assessment activities;
- using different types of classroom questioning and feedback in terms of tone, support and purpose as a course or programme unfolds.

Despite the progressive possibilities of techniques outlined here, it is important to reiterate the very powerful and distorting impact of pressures to meet the summative requirements of a qualification. This can lead to instrumental 'teaching to the test' or 'coaching to the criteria' and minimise deep engagement with criteria and standards as part of improving learning and motivation. Nevertheless, discussion of the role of diagnostic and formative assessment, together with a more strategic approach to including activities associated with them in a learning programme, may form part of a professional response to resisting these summative pressures.

Summary

Clarity about the diagnostic and formative purposes of assessment can form the basis for a more strategic and considered approach to assessment activities across a learning programme. Potentially, better uses of diagnostic and formative assessment enable institutions and individual teachers to identify good practice and learners to meet the requirements of a learning programme, hopefully in more motivated and engaged ways. However, lack of clarity about the purposes of diagnostic and formative assessment can generate information that might not be used productively, but which becomes instead onerous or generated merely to meet funding and retention targets. In addition, lack of clarity can result in teachers spending too much time on feedback that learners cannot use, or not seeing valuable classroom activities as sources of diagnosis and feedback.

References and further reading

Practical guidance for introducing diagnostic assessment and support systems in educational institutions
Martinex, P. (2000) *Improving student retention: a guide to successful strategies*. London: Further Education Development Agency.

Evaluation of potential for diagnostic and formative assessment to enhance learning
Black, P. and Wiliam, D. (2005) 'Developing a theory of formative assessment', in Gardner, J. (ed) (2005) *Assessment and Learning*. London: Sage Publications.

Black, P. (2005) 'The practice of assessment for learning in the classroom', in Garder, J. above.

Black, P. and Wiliam, D. (1998b) 'Assessment and classroom learning, Assessment' in *Education: Principles, Policy and Practice*, 5, 1, 1–78.

Broadfoot, P. (1999) 'Liberating the learner through assessment', in Collins, J. and Cooik, D. (eds) (1999) *Understanding Learning: influences and outcomes*. London: Paul Chapman Publishing/Open University.

Ecclestone, K. (2002) *Learning Autonomy in Post-16 Education: the policy and practice of formative assessment*. London: Routledge/ Falmer Press.

Gipps, C. (1994) *Beyond Testing: Towards a Theory of Educational Assessment*. London: Falmer Press.

Torrance, H. and Pryor, J. (1998) *Investigating Formative Assessment: Teaching Learning and Assessment in the Classroom*. Buckingham: Open University Press.

Strategies for improving classroom questioning:

Morgan, N. and Saxton, J. (1991) *Teaching, Questioning and Learning*. London: Routledge.

In-depth account of how a research project helped teachers to improve their formative assessment

Black, P., Harrison, C., Lee, C., Marshall, B. and Wiliam, D. (2004) *Assessment for Learning: putting it into practice*. Maidenhead: Open University Press.

CHAPTER 4

MOTIVATION, AUTONOMY AND LEARNING

Introduction

Many themes of this book are treated in a strongly technical way, aiming to offer advice and clarify underlying principles. As the previous chapters indicate, however, the design of assessment systems and their implementation are profoundly political and social in underlying purposes, trends and effects. When assessment is used well, it offers motivating ways for learners to describe achievement, to assess the quality of their own work and to set meaningful and useful targets. Political and social factors have a significant impact on the chances of realising these goals and many current trends in assessment have unintended, negative side effects. For example, highly competitive systems can demotivate those who do not get high grades, while the pressure of external targets can make teachers and students adopt a low-risk approach, thereby minimising engagement in order to 'get through' the requirements. In contrast to their aims of empowering learners, competence-based and outcome-based models appear often to create a tedious paper chase as part of accumulating evidence of achievement.

Recognising some of the tensions in principles and practices might enable practitioners and qualification designers to achieve their good intentions for assessment. An understanding of tensions also illuminates the limitations of particular assessment systems, which makes it important for institutions to consider how to achieve positive educational experiences within the constraints and contradictions of external requirements and increasingly prescriptive assessment models. Sound technical advice or rationales for change cannot reconcile this tension. Indeed, over-reliance on such advice can make it worse because it avoids proper debate about different beliefs and educational values implicit in all assessment systems. External guidance given to teachers also assumes that the professional development of new skills is easily amenable to didactic transmission of advice.

Such tensions are especially evident if we evaluate claims in the early 1990s that outcome-based assessment systems would offer a progressive basis for learning-related assessment and accreditation, particularly for learners who had not succeeded in old norm-referenced systems. The goals of improving motivation and increasing learners' autonomy have created numerous, rather bland claims about the role of assessment. Yet there are three main problems associated with claims about motivation, autonomy and learning. First, despite a large body of research into motivation, we have no clear conceptual basis for understanding the various types of motivation that different assessment systems may foster explicitly and implicitly. Second, there is no agreed conceptual basis for understanding the types of autonomy that learners might develop. Third, two competing models of learning and knowledge are implicit in official rhetoric about outcome-based models but also in teachers' everyday practice.

This chapter addresses these problems by exploring:

- different types of motivation within a formal learning programme;
- different types of autonomy that might be possible within a formal learning programme; and
- different ideas about learning.

1. Different types of motivation

There is a growing perception that the UK has a cultural problem of poor motivation for learning, yet ideas about motivation remain confused, particularly in relation to their implications for teaching and formative assessment. In part, confusion arises from a long-running distinction in cognitive psychology between:

- behaviourist perspectives that emphasise extrinsic motives based on external goals, performance rewards and short-term goals;
- humanist perspectives that offer a hierarchy of intrinsic motives for learning, based on the idea that people (particularly adults) have an innate desire to learn and develop; and
- cognitive perspectives that emphasise learners' tendencies to adopt preferred learning styles, or strategies, so that motivation increases if learners can work within their preferred styles.

A broad distinction between behaviourist and humanist research has produced unhelpful but enduring dichotomies between extrinsic and intrinsic motivation. For example, it is common for practitioners to contrast extrinsic motivation through compliance with targets and the use of reward and punishment unfavourably with intrinsic motivation that derives from a love of learning, the drive for mastery or feelings of civic and moral responsibility. Most educators regard intrinsic motivation as inherently desirable, while learners present a far more complex picture of their reasons for learning.

In addition to a dichotomy between extrinsic and intrinsic motivation, there is a tradition in cognitive psychologists that tends to emphasise *individual* traits, dispositions, attributes and responses and the need for teachers to diagnose and respond to them. This has led to a proliferation of learning styles tests and inventories which are supposed to diagnose and respond to 'preferred' styles and approaches to learning. Assumptions about learning styles and their importance are extremely problematic, despite their widespread appeal (see Coffeld *et al*, 2004a; 2004b).

One problem with discussion about motivation is that it overemphasises learners as individuals with largely fixed traits of behaviour. Much discussion about motivation also overlooks people's social and personal histories, social, cultural and family contexts and the power of social motivation. These factors are important for understanding motivation for learning. Broader conditions, such as changes to occupational structures, local job prospects and communal attitudes to learning, are also important influences on motivation (see, for example, Fevre *et al*, 1999; Rees *et al*, 2000; Zukas and Malcolm, 2000).

Instead of viewing motivation as an individual concern, it is perhaps more helpful to regard psychological factors, individual and group learning histories and social conditions as equally influential. This makes the effects of previous history and learning identity in shaping people's motivation an important professional concern. For example, motivation and achievement in formal learning programmes are both affected by:

- whether learners attribute achievement to factors outside their control (such as innate ability, difficulty with particular tasks and the effects of luck);
- intrinsic factors within their control, such as effort;
- learners' perceptions of job and social prospects in relation to the effort needed to succeed in formal learning; and
- learners' ideas about 'acceptable' behaviour within a learning programme.

Some researchers argue that these attributions are both individually and socially constructed and these reinforced in powerful but subtle ways through childhood experiences of formal assessment (see Torrance and Pryor, 1998; Reay and Wiliam, 1999). Research has also explored how formal education shapes children's learning identities and the ways in which young people weigh up their prospects in relation to educational opportunities (Ball *et al*, 2000; Pollard and Filer, 2000). Socialisation and the importance of local norms, peer attitudes to work and education all affect motivation in complex ways. For example, participating in formal learning can lead to emotional effects on adults' identities and senses of self in relation to their families and peers and to their motivation for deep engagement with learning (Brookfield, 2000).

This summary of motivation illuminates important connections between:
- individual motivation and the evolution of a personal learning identity;
- social, family and peer attitudes to learning and motivation;
- personality traits and dispositions (and the extent to which these are fluid or fixed); and
- the importance of different contexts and climates for learning.

Recognising individual, social and cultural factors in motivation suggests that we should avoid:
- portraying learners as having fixed or static dispositions, traits or learning styles;
- regarding assessment systems as only affecting individual motivation; assessment regimes also affect norms within groups and the types of responses that learners and teachers come to see as acceptable (see, for example, Ecclestone, 2002); and
- regarding external motivation and strategic approaches to learning as automatically undesirable: instead, they may be realistic and appropriate for some types of learning or at particular stages of a course (see Deci and Ryan, 2000).

Following arguments here, it is useful to be more precise about types of motivation by seeing them as part of a shifting continuum. Recent research by Manfred Prenzel and colleagues in Germany has explored the motivation of trainees in different vocational training programmes at work and in colleges over an extended period of time. This research reconciles the idea of strategic and external motivation and the powerful effects of self-determination and personal agency (Prenzel *et al*, 2001). It therefore offers useful categories for exploring individual and social aspects of motivation, and the different types of motivation that learners might develop during a course.

Prenzel and his colleagues draw from different psychological traditions to offer what they call "a systematically ordered spectrum of constructs" of motivation. These can be differentiated both in relation to behaviours and activities and to different educational contexts (Prenzel *et al*, *op cit*). The types are summarised here:

Amotivated

Learners lack any direction for motivation, and are, variously, indifferent or apathetic. Sometimes this state is almost permanent and therefore hard to shift or it appears at points during a course.

External

Learning takes place largely in association with reinforcement, reward, or to avoid threat or punishment. Short-term targets, prescriptive outcomes and criteria, frequent feedback and reviews of progress, deadlines, sanctions and grades can reinforce external motivation. This can be helpful at the beginning of a course, but if left unchecked, can become the main type of motivation all the way through.

Introjected

Learners 'internalise' an external supportive structure to help them get through the requirements of the course, such as the specifications offered to learners in outcome-based assessment systems, formal tutorial reviews and target-setting. These mechanisms enable learners to internalise the criteria for assessment and use them independently of teachers. Nevertheless, although introjected motivation is internal, it is not self-determined. For many learners who have been disaffected by assessment in the past, introjected motivation is powerful and, initially, empowering. However, like external motivation, it can become a straitjacket if it underpins learning throughout the whole of a course.

Identified

Learning occurs when students accept content or activities which may hold no incentive in terms of processes or content (they might even see them as a burden) but which are necessary and important in attaining a particular pre-defined goal such as a qualification or more short-term targets. It links closely to introjected motivation.

Intrinsic

Learners perceive any incentives to be gained as being intrinsic to the content or processes involved in a formal learning or assessment activity. This form of motivation accords with humanist ideas of learning for its own sake or to meet goals of mastery and social responsibilities and commitments. It is often more prevalent amongst learners than practitioners might assume and takes idiosyncratic and sometimes fleeting forms.

Interested

Learners do not merely recognise the intrinsic value of particular activities but also assign subjective and meaningful attributes to the skill or process of learning. Learners who show this type of motivation fuse their sense of self with the identity of being a learner through the requirements of a course and relationships with peers and teachers. Like intrinsic motivation, this is often idiosyncratic, very personal and assessed by learners ipsatively.

Attributes associated with interested motivation relate strongly to the positive notions of learning or personal identities that Ball *et al* found to be integral to the processes and experiences in young people's lives of 'becoming somebody'. For these young adults, formal education played an important but not dominant part in their evolving identity (Ball *et al*, *op cit*; see also Crossan *et al*, 2001). Interested motivation therefore relates closely to Maslow's notion of 'self-actualisation', where one's identity, learning activities, feelings of social and civic responsibility and personal development are fused together (Maslow, 1987).

The strength of a fluctuating spectrum of ordered constructs is that it mixes different psychological ideas about motivation and does not polarise extrinsic and instrinsic motives as fixed individual traits, or 'desirable' and 'undesirable' types of motivation. The idea of a spectrum or continuum of motivation also suggests the possibility of being much more strategic about motivation within learning programmes than is usually the case. For example, the psychodynamic notion of 'introjection' enables teachers to use formal support structures at the beginning of a learning programme but does not prevent them from trying to encourage or exploit learners' intrinsic, or interested motivation as the basis for a positive personal and learning identity.

It is therefore useful to see motivational states as:
- fluctuating across a spectrum of extrinsic and intrinsic types during the progress of a course or programme; for example they might be strategic and low-level at some points of the course but necessarily deep and intrinsic at other points;
- influenced by individual traits, habits and preferences in learning and study, but also by social and cultural factors; and
- springboards for other forms of motivation; for example, an assessment system may encourage external, introjected and

identified motivation as a springboard for intrinsic, interested motivation.

The categories here provide a basis for being more realistic about motivation and for recognising that strategic forms of external, introjected and identified motivation need not necessarily be negative. Being clearer about types of motivation however also requires explicit expectations from course designers, practitioners and learners that certain skills and attributes might demand intrinsic and interested motivation at different points of a course or learning programme. Using a spectrum of categories might therefore enable teachers to help learners make positive links between their personal and learning identities and learning and assessment activities.

2. Types of autonomy

There has been much rhetoric about learners' autonomy. Terms like 'independence', 'empowerment' and 'autonomy' are often used vaguely in political, academic and professional discussion about the goals of lifelong learning. There is not space to do justice to the complexity of the different meanings of autonomy in education, but a brief review shows that it often encompasses an interchangeable use of 'independent learning', 'taking responsibility for one's own learning', 'self-determination' and 'self-regulation' (Boud, 1988). From a liberal, individualistic perspective which is prevalent in Western cultures, autonomy might, for example, be seen as:

- a general *goal* of education, enabling an individual to be independent from external authority and "free from disabling conflicts" in one's personality and to act and work as s/he chooses (Gibbs quoted by Boud, 1988, p18-19);
- the ability to think critically, in order to act autonomously to define what is morally acceptable, to choose alternatives between conflicting ideas, to have a 'mind of one's own' (Dearden, quoted by Boud, *op cit*, p19).

From this perspective, autonomy becomes both a goal and a set of processes for realising it. Rooted in Greek notions of political self-government, meritocracy and democratic citizenship based on free but socially committed and fulfilled individuals, liberal humanist notions of 'self-determination' and 'self-actualisation' all underpin contemporary versions of these ideals in many Western societies, particularly in Europe and North America. It is important to note that Eastern and other non-Western cultures may have quite different notions of autonomy that are both implicit and overt in their education systems.

Some psychologists portray autonomy as:

- a cognitive process that might be directed towards goals of critical thinking and acting but which might also address learning activities and their effectiveness; or
- tacit and overt meta-cognitive processes for planning, monitoring and reviewing one's learning (often referred to as 'self-regulation').

These cognitive processes are integral to intrinsic motivation and deep engagement with the content and processes of learning within a particular subject (Newton, 2000). Some researchers go further and suggest that adults develop a self-conscious capacity to 'know how they know what they know' and also to employ practical logic to new situations, based on experience (Broofield, 2000). These capabilities are, Brookfield argues, distinctive characteristics of adults' autonomy as learners. Carl Rogers links goals of democratic liberal humanism to these psychological processes to argue for a radical, naturalistic approach where learners are free to determine, set, carry out and assess their own goals (Rogers, 1983). A humanist view of adults' innate drive to learn has been particularly influential in American and British adult education.

Much current discussion about 'autonomy' in post-16 education however often focuses on a technical meaning of autonomy as:

- a procedure or method, such as action planning, setting targets and reviewing progress;
- flexible access to resources and facilities (for example, web-based materials, modular structures, open and distance learning);
- independence to work outside the requirements of formal structures and didactic teaching.

In the light of the other meanings of autonomy as summarised above, it is important to evaluate what type of autonomy might be overtly or implicitly evident in an assessment system. The typology summarised here has been applied to the types of autonomy shown by GNVQ students in FE colleges (see Ecclestone, 2002). It focuses on the autonomy that formal learning programmes and their summative and formative assessment methods may develop or inhibit in learners, both overtly and unwittingly.

The typology proposes that autonomy can be *procedural* (technical); *personal* (practical – as in one's own 'practice'); *critical* and, ultimately, *emancipatory*. It relates autonomy to three different models of teaching and learning: *transmission*, *transaction* or *transformation*. The typology also suggests that there is overlap and fluctuation between different motivations and forms of autonomy during a learning programme and that different formative assessment practices may encourage one type of autonomy more than another.

Procedural autonomy

This might comprise:

- some control over pace, timing and content of study and assessed work;
- opportunities to negotiate types of learning activities and 'appropriate' evidence of achievement; and
- the chance to be more proactive within specified rules, outcomes and assessment criteria.

Procedural autonomy encourages:

- confidence in using techniques or processes or a body of technical or specialist language independently;
- transmission of pre-defined outcomes, knowledge, processes and content by teachers, or through open learning and computer-based materials;
- transaction over how tasks might be done;
- the likelihood of an emphasis on external and introjected motivation; and
- teacher- and self-assessment that focuses on checking that criteria are met while rewarding short-term goals and the replication of information.

A likely side effect is superficial engagement with requirements in order to get through the criteria. In addition, if procedural autonomy is the only goal of an assessment system and is underpinned by external, introjected or identified motivation, it becomes little more than an imposed technical empowerment that is far from progressive.

Nevertheless, overt attention to learners' procedural autonomy may be important at the beginning of learning programmes. Confidence with procedures, systems and the technical language underpinning particular subjects enables future confidence with more sophisticated forms of planning, new activities or the concepts behind terminology and perhaps the contested nature of the rules themselves. There may also be a necessary progression from learners' abilities to make decisions with the support of prescribed procedures and their subsequent ability to judge when it is, or is not, needed. Procedural autonomy may therefore be a prerequisite or a co-requisite for more sophisticated forms of personal and critical autonomy.

Personal (practical) autonomy

Humanist ideas that people have an innate drive to become self-directing suggest another form of autonomy. Personal autonomy derives from knowledge of one's strengths and weaknesses, learning habits and potential choices for action and progression. These insights might be the beginning of a 'repertoire of responses' discussed above as the basis for autonomy as self-actualisation. Yet personal autonomy within occupational or pro-fessional practice cannot be isolated from recognising and dealing with the ethical and moral dilemmas that this practice raises.

Engagement with moral and ethical issues might therefore enhance self-knowledge and the ability to make moral choices in relation to professional and occupational practice. For example, the goal in this book of raising underlying tensions and dilemmas in assessment is perhaps an example of aiming to develop readers' personal autonomy in relation to their professional role in assessment. As discussion below shows, this aim is inextricably linked to critical autonomy.

The typology proposes that personal autonomy is situated within a particular learning or subject context, underpinned by identified, intrinsic and, ideally, interested motivation. Its development also requires:

- learners and teachers to attribute achievement to effort and engagement;
- good relationships and transaction between teachers and peers;
- negotiation of intended outcomes and how to achieve them;
- emphasis on positive interdependence among learners and co-operative approaches to problem-setting and problem-solving; and
- negotiated processes of assessment, review and recording of achievement.

Unless personal autonomy is related to procedural and critical autonomy, it is prone to reductionist equations with procedural autonomy. Ultimately, people's ability to go beyond an awareness of their strengths and weaknesses within a set of procedures, or to get past a preoccupation with their personal attributes, is shaped by the ability to appraise their position within a wider context. The ability to 'think otherwise' makes it difficult to separate personal autonomy from learners' broader life chances and the socio-economic and cultural conditions affecting these chances.

Critical autonomy

For a significant number of educators, critical autonomy is the ultimate goal of education and of a democratic citizenship that encourages critical intelligence. In higher education, for example, critical autonomy is seen to emerge through subject expertise, where students engage with established bodies of thought and participate in associated conversations with teachers and peers. Such processes and commitments can develop an understanding beyond conventional insights and wisdom.

From a more radical tradition, learners "participate in determining the content of learning, or what counts as educational knowledge" (Young cited by Bates, 1998, p. 11). For some adults in higher education, critical autonomy is inseparable from their social and cultural needs and a desire to contribute actively to their deprived communities. These goals demand intellectual depth and the ability to make connections between ideas (Ross, 1995). The ability to think critically is therefore integral to critical and personal autonomy but critical thinking is not synonymous with either form of autonomy.

It is important to be precise about where critical autonomy is important for learning a vocational subject or skill or for coping with a job or life, and where it might simply be a desirable goal within formal education. Without this precision, designers of vocational qualifications might regard calls for critical autonomy as little more than 'academic drift' in courses where learners might not want or need it. Without discussion about when critical autonomy might *not* be necessary, its promotion tends to attract worthy but vacuous proselytising.

However, if critical autonomy *is* a legitimate goal for assessment within a learning programme, it is important to recognise barriers to its development. For example, there are different interpretations of 'critical'. There are also particular cultures of academic or vocational subjects, professions or occupations where certain forms of critical thinking and autonomy are accepted and valued. In other contexts, critical autonomy is seen as undesirable or unacceptable. Such tensions can be particularly traumatic for adults 'becoming critical' through educational experiences, where peers or family may resent this new attribute (Brookfield, 2000). In addition, if critical autonomy means a critique of one's own position, to challenge or even transform situations collectively, it is important to question how far it is realistic to hope that prescriptive assessment models can promote critical autonomy. Finally, it is important to recognise that critical autonomy may take many years and specialist expertise to develop and that it often disappears temporarily when learners confront a new subject domain.

In relation to learning and assessment activities to develop critical autonomy, the typology proposes the following:

- *transaction* and *transformation* that build upon problem-solving and collaboration within a particular subject or occupational context;
- a belief that knowledge is dynamic, uncertain and contestable;
- diverse activities, formal and informal discourses, openness and creativity within a community of practice; and
- constructive, self-regulating processes that enable learners to assess their own knowledge and processes of learning.

Diagnostic and formative assessment needs to:

- encourage critical reflection and engagement with dilemmas in subject disciplines, and in social- and occupationally-related problems;
- offer learners oral and written 'critical conversations' that encourage them to assess their own work and relate its quality to that of peers and immediate superiors;
- develop resilience in accepting critical or negative feedback;
- build the confidence needed to transform feedback into a more sophisticated critical understanding; and
- help learners know how to interpret teachers' often idiosyncratic comments about their work and then to use them proactively to improve future work.

These techniques therefore extend the idea of formative assessment as merely feedback and review. Instead, formative assessment includes questions for understanding (or to diagnose barriers to understanding), creating climates where people feel able to challenge or to ask curriculum-related questions of each other and teachers, and strategic debriefing of learning processes with students.

Types of motivation and autonomy are re-evaluated in the final chapter in relation to how different assessment activities at different stages of a learning programme might foster or inhibit them. An explicit focus on promoting deeper forms of motivation and autonomy is crucial to an organisational strategy for assessment.

3. Tensions and controversies in ideas about learning

It is possible to identify two different, contradictory models of learning within most assessment systems in post-16 education. Broadly, these can be characterised as *constructivist* and *positivist* ideas about the nature of knowledge and thereby about learning and assessment. These ideas and beliefs are almost always implicit and are rarely the focus for discussion among practitioners and learners about motivation, autonomy and learning. This section summarises the main themes in these models.

Constructivist models

A constructivist view of knowledge and learning encompasses the following ideas:
- that knowledge is situated within specific contexts and communities of practice;
- that individuals and groups construct and reconstruct knowledge within those contexts;
- that knowledge and skills are not fixed or easily measurable and replicable; and
- that learning and assessment processes and activities are rooted in particular forms of co-operation and social interaction.

These ideas shift a long-running emphasis in educational psychology on cognitive processes and the conceptual structures of individuals to the ecology and sociology of specific learning groups and organisational cultures (see, for example, Lave and Wenger, 1991). Constructivist notions of learning therefore emphasise social and cultural dimensions within specific communities of practice, and the social and cultural factors that hinder or facilitate people's entry and participation in them.

There are attempts to translate constructivist concepts of knowledge and learning into assessment techniques. For example, Vygotsky's concept of 'zones of proximal development', has been widely interpreted as a technique for encouraging teachers and more expert peers amongst students and the wider community to work collaboratively with less expert learners. It has also led to ideas about 'scaffolding' tasks and questions in an attempt to close the gap between where learners are, the work they can produce with help from a teacher or a more expert peer, and achievement of the desired standard. The aim is to help learners internalise the standard of work implied in the criteria and to appreciate what it means to 'close the gap'. Feedback moves from detailed support to more general advice or questions as learners gain confidence and expertise in translating feedback into improvements and new goals (see, for example, Gipps, 1994; Black and Wiliam *op cit*).

Positivist models

In contrast to constructivist ideas about learning and knowledge, a positivist view proposes:
- that knowledge and skills are definable, observable, teachable and therefore measurable;
- that people's behaviour can be both conditioned and modified through stimulus and response, reward and punishment; and
- that clear specifications of objectives offer a 'transparent' basis for assessment.

In education, these positivist notions were particularly prominent through the behavioural objectives movement between the 1930s and 1960s. Other strands of psychology have aimed to explore cognitive development and to operationalise this development through strategies such as personality testing and inventories for learning styles, or to derive learning objectives from precise study of human behaviour in different contexts. Bloom's taxonomy of cognitive objectives, for example, has been extremely influential in the design of mainstream qualifications both here and in the United States, based on the claim that it defines a systematic hierarchy of psychological processes for acquiring and processing knowledge (Bloom, 1956; Anderson *et al*, 1998).

There have been criticisms that a positivist view of knowledge and learning leads to:
- programmed instruction and step by step learning, with passive recipients rather than active participants;
- 'surface learning' and instrumental compliance with targets;
- constraints on teachers and students constructing their own curriculum; and
- attempts to eliminate uncertainty and creativity in learning and to atomise and fragment knowledge.

A particular problem in recognising if positivist or constructivist ideas underpin different techniques and activities is that a description of an activity and its accompanying rationale could derive from either model of learning. This problem is evident in outcome-based assessment models where constructivist language and aims underpin both the rationale for outcome-based assessment and the activities involved.

Learning and assessment in an outcome-based model

Early versions of outcome-based assessment attempted to put into practice the positivist belief that: "if you cannot say what you require [from students], how are you going to develop it and how do you know when you've achieved it?" (Jessup quoted by Burke, *op cit*, p. 60). This belief was criticised as the 'Holy Grail' of transparent and explicit specifications of outcomes (see Hyland, 1994; Wolf, 1995). However, supporters of outcome-based assessment did appear to address warnings that the very notion of outcomes was inimical to learning processes that foster creativity, skill and enduring motivation to learn. They claimed that assessment is demystified if learners know the outcomes they can gain and the criteria by which they are assessed. Far from imposing a curriculum straitjacket, supporters argued that specifications freed learners and teachers to determine their own pedagogy and assessment activities. In addition, the GNVQ embedded processes of self-directed learning and self-assessment within the grading criteria as a means of motivating students to address these skills (see Burke, 1995).

In summary, supporters of criterion or outcome-based assessment claim that it:

- is democratic and motivating because it publicly defines outcomes and criteria for assessing achievement;
- enables learners and teachers to negotiate learning processes and evidence that might comprise achievement and progress;
- promotes learner autonomy in the form of choice over assessment activities and processes;
- makes standards of assessment more valid and authentic by specifying the outcomes and criteria that comprise the required knowledge, skills and attributes; and
- offers a basis for merging vocational and academic pathways and credit-based qualifications.

Claims and counter-claims illustrate that outcome-based models incorporate loose constructivist images of individual learning targets, processes and activities, and evidence of achievement. In theory, these are constructed between teachers and learners around pre-defined outcomes and situated within specific local contexts. Other constructivist notions appear in the idea that developing intrinsic and interested motivation comes from growing confidence and opportunities to negotiate learning processes and assessment evidence.

One problem is that such ideas sit uneasily with forms of external introjected and identified motivation that are encouraged through pre-defined targets, structures and criteria. In addition, positivist and behaviourist overtones are evident in the idea that outcomes and criteria for assessment can be derived from observing everyday behaviours and skills so that learners can generate evidence of competence. A further difficulty in evaluating the effects of outcome-based systems is that many of their critics espouse open-ended, constructivist notions of knowledge and learning and appear to reject any positivist basis for learning. There is also a tendency among critics to blame outcome-based assessment for atomised or instrumental approaches to learning without recognising external factors that lead to instrumental forms of motivation. As the first section shows above, important social and cultural factors affect motivation and constructions of knowledge within a post-16 education. Students' commitment to a 'community of practice', for example, is affected by whether they want to be part of peer group norms or whether outside influences such as family and colleagues value the learning they are taking part in.

Responses to assessment activities are also shaped by self-perceptions of learning abilities and identities and expectations of achievement. For example, deeply-held but implicit expectations also emerge through behaviourist practices within schools. One effect is that extrinsic motivation based on rewards, performance goals and punishments is deeply entrenched in teachers' and students' assessment practices and experiences (see Torrance and Pryor, 1998). As discussion above shows, previous learning careers and identities, shaped in response to increasingly rigid assessment in the National Curriculum, are essential variables in motivation and responses to different assessment systems.

A positivist tradition is also exacerbated by pressures on teachers to get as many pupils as possible through external tests while minimising the demotivation of those who do not succeed. Similar pressures are evident in post-compulsory education where teachers want to maximise students' achievement in order to give them the best chance possible in difficult socio-economic circumstances. This can encourage a narrow view of what constitutes 'purposeful' learning.

Summary

Conflicting goals embedded within early models of outcome-based assessment were not well articulated in relation to theories of learning. Nevertheless, it is apparent from discussion in this chapter that few, if any, learning programmes or qualifications have a coherent model of learning!

Dichotomies between types of motivation and autonomy or models of knowledge within learning programmes are also far from clear-cut. Practitioners, qualification designers and learners often talk about motivation and autonomy but can mean quite different things. In addition, complex theories of knowledge and learning cannot be reduced to simple assessment and teaching techniques. Such tensions make it too simplistic to dismiss outcome-based models as offering little more than an impoverished form of behaviourism. It is also inappropriate to allow vague claims that outcome-based models enable construction and negotiation of a learning programme to go unchallenged.

The chapter has offered a typology for categorising different types of motivation and autonomy. This might be used as a basis for thinking strategically about how teachers within particular subject disciplines and occupational areas might encourage different forms of motivation and autonomy. It is apparent that distinctions between types of motivation and autonomy, as well as between models of learning and knowledge, are neither explicit or understood in any assessment regime. These problems suggest a need to differentiate clearly between the effects on motivation and autonomy of a particular assessment model, institutional and structural factors, students' dispositions to learning and their expectations of progression and achievement.

References and further reading

Analysis of a systematic hierarchy of cognitive skills in learning

Anderson, L. W. (1997) *Rethinking Bloom's Taxonomy: Implications for Learning and Assessment*. Columbia: University of South Carolina.

Bloom, B. (1956) *A Taxonomy of Cognitive Objectives*. New York: Mackay.

Accounts of children's, young learners' and adults' identities and motivation

Ball, S. Maguire, M. and Macrae, S. (2000) *Choice, Pathways and Transitions Post-16: New Youth, New Economics in the Global City.* London: Routledge/Falmer Press.

Bloomer, M. (1997) *Curriculum-making in Post-16 education: The Social Conditions of Studentship.* London: Routledge.

Bloomer, M. and Hodkinson, P. (1997) *Moving into FE: the Voice of the Learner.* London: Further Education Development Agency.

Bloomer, M. and Hodkinson, P. (1999) *College Life: the Voice of the Learner.* London: Further Education Development Agency.

Brookfield, S. (2000) 'Adult cognition as a dimension of lifelong learning', in Field, J. and Leicester, M.(eds) (2000) *Lifelong Learning Across the Lifespan.* London: Routledge/Falmer Press.

Crossan, B., Field, J., Gallacher, J. and Merrill, B. (2001) 'Understanding participation in learning for non-traditional adult learners: learning careers and the construction of learning identities', *British Journal of Sociology of Education*, 24, 1, 55–67.

Ecclestone, K. and Pryor, J. (2003) 'Learning careers or assessment careers? The impact of assessment systems on learning', *British Educational Research Journal*, 29, 4, 471–487.

Ecclestone, K. (2002) *Learning Autonomy in Post-16 Education: the policy and practice of formative assessment.* London: Routledge/Falmer Press.

Ecclestone, K. (2004) 'Learning in a comfort zone: cultural and social capital in outcome-based assessment regimes', *Assessment in Education*, 11, 1, 29–47.

Pollard, A. and Filer, A. (1999) *The Social World of Pupil Career: Strategic Biographies through Primary School.* London: Cassell.

Reay, D. and Wiliam, D. (1999) ' "I'll be a nothing": Structure, Agency and the Construction of Identity through Assessment', *British Educational Research Journal*, 25, 3, 343–355.

Rees, G., Fevre, R. and Gorrard, S. (1997) 'History, Place and the Learning Society: Towards a Sociology of Lifetime Learning', *Journal of Education Policy*, 12, 6, 485–498.

Torrance, H. and Pryor, J. (1998) *Investigating Formative Assessment.* Buckingham: Open University Press.

Zukas, M. and Malcom, J. (2000) *Pedagogies for lifelong learning: Building Bridges or Building Walls?* Paper given to Supporting Lifelong Learning Colloquium. London, University of East London, 4 July, 2000.

General theories of learning and motivation

Deci, E. and Ryan, R. (1999) 'A Meta-analytic View of Experiments Examining the Effects of Extrinsic Rewards on Intrinsic Motivation', *Psychological Bulletin*, 126, 6, 627–688.

Dweck, C. S. (2000) *Self-Theories: Their Role in Motivation, Personality and Development*. Philadelphia: Taylor Francis Psychology Press.

Haywood, R. (1997) 'Links between learning styles, teaching methods and course requirements', in Edwards, T., Fitzgibbon, C., Hardman, F., Haywood, R., and Meagher, N. (1997) *Separate but equal?: GNVQs and A-levels*. London: Routledge.

Lave, J. and Wenger, E. (1991) *Situated Learning: Legitimate Peripheral Participation*. Cambridge: Cambridge University Press.

Newton, D. (2000) *Teaching for Understanding*. London: Falmer Press.

Prenzel, M., Kramer, K. and Dreschel, B. (2001) 'Self-interested and Interested Learning in Vocational Education', in Beck, K. (2001) (ed.) *Teaching-Learning Processes in Initial Business Education*. Boston: Kluwer.

Theories and critiques of outcome-based assessment

Bates, I. (1998) 'Resisting 'Empowerment and Realising Power: An Exploration of Aspects of the GNVQ' in *Journal of Education and Work*, 11, 2, 187–205.

Bloomer, M. (1998): ' "They tell you what to do and then they let you get on with it": Illusions of Progressivism in GNVQ' in *Journal of Education and Work*, 11, 2, 167–187

Burke, J. (ed.) (1995) *Outcomes Learning and the Curriculum: Implications for NVQs GNVQs and Other Qualifications*. London: Falmer Press.

Hyland, T. (1994) *Competence, Education and NVQs*. London: Cassell.

Jessup, G. (1991) *Outcomes: NVQs and the Emerging Model of Education and Training*. London: Falmer Press.

McNair, S. (1995) 'Outcomes and autonomy' in Burke, J. (ed.) (1995) *Outcomes, Learning and the Curriculum: Implications for NVQs, GNVQs and Other Qualifications*. London: Falmer Press.

Pollard, A. (1985) *The Social World of the Primary School*. London: Holt, Rinehart and Winston.

Critique of the negative impact of summative assessment on learning and motivation among adults

Rogers, C. (1983) *Freedom to Learn for the 1980s*. New York: Merrill and Company.

Discussion of broader goals of adult education

Ross, C. (1995) 'Seizing the Quality Initiative: Regeneration and the Radical Project', in Thompson, J. and Mayo, M. (eds) (1995) *Adult Learning, Critical Intelligence and Social Change*. Leicester: NIACE.

Discussion of learner autonomy

Boud, D. (1988) *Developing Student Autonomy in Learning*. London, Kogan Page.

Ecclestone, cited above.

Theories, principles and evaluations of learning styles

Coffield, F., Moseley, D., Hall, E. and Ecclestone, K. (2004a) *Learning styles: a systematic and critical review*. London, Learning and Skills Development Agency.

Coffield, F., Moseley, D., Hall, E. and Ecclestone, K. (2004b) *Learning styles: what has research to say to practice?* London, Learning and Skills Development Agency (www.lsda.org.uk).

CHAPTER 5

PROCEDURES AND PRACTICES IN DIFFERENT QUALIFICATION SYSTEMS

Introduction

The previous chapters have aimed to offer a basis for understanding the diverse processes and procedures that awarding bodies and the QCA require post-16 institutions and teachers to take part in and implement. Yet many teachers in different organisations either experience a number of procedures, depending on which awarding bodies they use to offer a particular qualification, or they are familiar with the ethos and practices of one system. This can make it difficult to recognise different goals embedded within these procedures, and for institutions to co-ordinate procedures between different awarding bodies' requirements.

The large number of awarding bodies that an institution might be dealing with adds further confusion. For example, a further education college may have higher education courses validated by a university. These will use external examiners employed by the university to examine students' work and 'peer reviewers' employed on a part-time basis by the Quality Assurance Agency to evaluate the quality of programmes and visit teachers, students and institutional managers involved in them. A college also offers diverse qualifications that used to be accredited either by subject examining boards or vocational awarding bodies but which are now likely to be offered by the new unitary bodies. Set up by the Department for Education and Employment (DfEE) in 1997, these are a merger of GCSE and GCE A-level examination boards with vocational bodies. Where these bodies offer qualifications within the QCA's national qualification framework, they are required to implement quality assurance and assessment procedures regulated by the QCA (see below).

In addition, as discussion of validity, reliability and standards showed in Chapter Two, there is confusion about the difference between quality assurance and quality control and the respective roles of officials from awarding bodies, the Learning and Skills Council and inspection bodies, the Adult Learning Inspectorate (ALI) and the Office for Standards in Education (OFSTED). Each organisation and individuals within it also tend to use the terms discussed in this chapter loosely or interchangeably with other terms.

With different traditions and ethos, it is possible, despite diverse procedures and qualifications, to discern common practices and aims and it can be useful to identify overlap, similarity and difference between them. This chapter:

- defines and lists some of the main awarding bodies in the post-16 education and training system;
- defines 'accreditation' and the accompanying processes within mainstream qualification systems in which teachers and institutional managers need to take part; and
- outlines relevant questions that teachers and institutional managers may wish to ask in considering which accreditation or certification system to use with particular groups of learners.

1. Awarding bodies

Unlike many other countries, Britain has no national system to control the setting up of examining or awarding bodies. Anyone can offer examinations and issue certificates but these are more likely to be recognised by others as a useful qualification if organisations are authorised to offer accreditation through royal charter (such as universities), a government directive or a request from institutions or other bodies. There are many organisations offering accreditation or certification, including an increasing number of professional bodies and commercial organisations such as Microsoft. The term 'awarding body' is therefore used here to cover the whole range of agencies offering formal recognition of achievement.

The history and organisational ethos of each awarding body reflects various traditions in different sectors of education and training, in the acquisition of craft and apprenticeship skills, and in professional recruitment and development. Concern about diverse accreditation processes, *ad hoc* and incoherent levels attached to qualifications, and about the relevance of qualifications to occupational requirements and the expressed needs of employers, led to the setting up of the National Council for Vocational Qualifications (NCVQ) in 1986. This was intended to rationalise all vocational qualifications, covering 80 per cent of the workforce, into a national framework by 1992. NCVQ also introduced General National Vocational Qualifications in 1992 as the basis for rationalising all general vocational qualifications (GNVQs were relaunched as Advanced Vocational Certificates of Education (AVCEs) in 2000).

Further strategies to rationalise arrangements for assessment and qualifications were attempted in 1997 when the NCVQ was merged with the Schools and Curriculum Assessment Authority to form the Qualifications and Curriculum Authority (QCA). In the same year, the three main awarding bodies for vocational qualifications (City & Guilds, the Business and Technology Council (BTEC) and RSA Examinations Board (RSA) were merged with the largest examination boards for general education in GCSEs and A-levels to form unitary bodies (see below). So far, rationalisation does not seem to have eliminated the confusion addressed in this chapter, although there has been some harmonisation of procedures. Currently, the QCA regulates procedures and formats for assessment in any qualification that an awarding body wishes to place in the national qualifications framework. This is leading to increased homogenisation of summative assessment methods and questions about why the UK system needs so many awarding bodies.

Bodies offering accreditation may also undertake processes associated with the validation, moderation, verification and certification of learning programmes. (All these terms are discussed below.) However, each awarding body has different requirements and degrees of their official involvement in these processes. Although all awarding bodies specify assessment and examination arrangements, as well as criteria for validating a programme or centre, some also require centres to promote certain principles of learning, teaching quality, programme content and assessment methods. The scope and remit of the different bodies therefore vary considerably, as does knowledge amongst employers, teachers and learners about what the different credits or qualifications represent in terms of content and currency.

National awarding bodies

Organisations involved in the accreditation of adult learning, both within national accreditation systems and through individual qualifications, include:
- Business and Technology Education Council (BTEC) as part of the EdExcel Foundation (BTEC and the University of London

examinations board formed one of the three unitary bodies set up in 1997.

- The Assessment and Qualifications Alliance (AQA) is the largest of the three unitary bodies. It initially comprised City & Guilds, the Associated Examining Board and the Northern Examinations and Assessment Board. City & Guilds reverted to its own independent brand in 1999);
- OCR is a unitary body formed from the Oxford and Cambridge examination boards and the RSA Examinations Board. Contrary to popular perception, the RSA separated completely from the Royal Society of Arts in 1983;
- Open College Networks (OCNs);
- NCFE (this was formerly the Northern Council for Further Education) an awarding body for qualifications and certificates in further, adult and community education; and
- individual universities are awarding bodies for their own degrees under royal charter. They may franchise part of their awards to other institutions, such as colleges or workplaces, and sometimes work in partnership schemes to offer awards, again with colleges or workplaces.

Examining boards

Examining boards are also responsible for the design of syllabi and the setting of examinations for academic and vocational awards such as A-levels and GCSEs. In 1997, the main examination boards were merged with vocational awarding bodies to become unitary bodies (see above). Other examples are the Joint Matriculation Board and the Southern Examining Group.

Professional bodies

A large number of professional bodies offer their own accreditation and increasingly validate centres to run courses and programmes in further, higher and adult education. Among these are:

- Nursery Nursing Examining Board (NNEB);
- Construction Industry Training Board (CITB);
- Chartered Institute of Personnel Development (CIPD); and
- Engineering Training Authority (ETA).

Sometimes, organisations and institutions offer accreditation for programmes leading to professional awards that are carried out in conjunction with an awarding body. For example, a university validates the training offered by Sotheby's while other awarding bodies, such as BTEC, OCNs, City & Guilds and RSA validate programmes for specific companies and organisations.

Membership bodies

Some membership bodies also validate courses and learning programmes such as:

- trades unions;
- National Association of Citizens Advice Bureaux;
- chambers of commerce; and
- National Federation of Women's Institutes.

Open College Networks

OCNs are locally based and controlled networks which operate within a national framework provided through the National Open College Network (NOCN). They offer accreditation for locally-designed programmes based in workplaces, the community, voluntary organisations or colleges. OCNs award credits and certificates for achievement on their recognised programmes.

National Qualifications Framework

A growing number of certificated programmes and qualifications that enable someone to practise a craft or profession, or to progress further in the education and training system, compete for inclusion in the National Qualifications Framework (NQF), which is regulated by the QCA. Although there is confusion about the difference between a certificate of achievement and a qualification, any formally recognised programme that an awarding body wants to place in the NQF must conform to a code of practice on quality assurance and quality control, and to certain stipulations about summative assessment.

The current NQF offers qualifications at different levels, based on broad notions about 'parity of esteem' between equivalent qualifications at each level – see Figure 4.

Figure 4.

Level of qualification	General		Vocationally-related	Occupational
5 4	Higher-level qualifications BTEC Higher Nationals			Level 5 NVQ Level 4 NVQ
3 advanced level	A level	Free-standing mathematics units level 3	Vocational A level (Advanced GNVQ)	Level 3 NVQ
2 intermediate level	GCSE grade A*–C	Free-standing mathematics units level 2	intermediate GNVQ	Level 2 NVQ
1 foundation level	GCSE grade D–G	Free-standing mathematics units level 1	Foundation GNVQ	Level 1 NVQ
Entry level	Entry level certificate			

2. Processes associated with accreditation and certification

For the purposes of understanding the procedures used in qualifications, it is helpful to regard 'accreditation' as a process of formally recognising and awarding credit for learning achievement. This meaning encompasses diverse procedures, from allowing a centre to run a course and any related assessment activities, to processes for quality assurance and quality control. Accreditation therefore involves processes of formative and summative assessment, but also procedures to gain approval to run particular courses and assure their quality.

However, the term is also used to describe other processes in the education and training system. For example, some awarding bodies refer to 'accredited' institutions as those that have been through certain quality assurance procedures in order to be able to offer their pro– grammes and qualifications. 'Accreditation' can also refer to the process of confirming the right to professional practice or to the practice under the now-defunct Further Education Funding Council of offering further education colleges with high inspection grades the status of 'accredited colleges' and thereby a 'lighter touch' inspection regime. In this chapter, the term 'accreditation' refers to the whole set of interlocking processes that organisations and awarding bodies use to recognise and certify learning achievement.

In qualification systems, accreditation involves judgments about the value of learning: this value may be expressed as a grade, or a record of credits achieved. Traditionally, this has been done by scrutinising the content, delivery, methods of assessment and the intended outcomes of learning and then attributing a value to the learning through an award or qualification. As section one showed, a range of organisations and agencies offer accreditation, such as national awarding and examining bodies, an examining board, a higher education institution, a professional body or an OCN. The various processes involved in accreditation can be carried out in formal, institutional frameworks (such as FE colleges or university), but accreditation is also increasingly available in work-based training, adult and community education services, private training organisations and companies.

Credit

Accreditation involves a notion of value which may be implicit or explicit. In credit-based systems, this is made clear to the learner and quantified through the awarding of credits but confusion arises because the term 'credit' is either used generically within a particular system or to quantify learning. Credit can also be sometimes used to describe a grade of achievement e.g. pass/credit/distinction.

In systems based on a precise definition, credit is a unit of value, which may be attached to a number of outcomes of learning. Some accreditation systems attach a credit value to the actual or notional amount of time taken to achieve learning outcomes, while other credits may be solely outcome-based regardless of the time taken to gain them. In systems without a precise definition of outcomes, credit usually refers to a unit of delivery in the form of a module or other package of learning.

Credits are therefore derived in different ways. The credit accumulation and transfer system (CATS), used in many universities, derives credits by dividing up a full-time degree into 360 credits, 120 at Level One, 120 at Level Two and 120 at Level Three. Increasing numbers of universities also have detailed level descriptors that show how learning outcomes at the three levels develop and build up to an honours degree.

The OCNs, on the other hand, base the award of credits on outcomes achievable in 30 hours of notional learning time. The term 'credit' is used differently in NVQs where the awarding of an NVQ unit is based on the achievement of specified occupational outcomes regardless of the time taken or where the learning took place.

In all accreditation systems, small, manageable components (sometimes referred to as modules or units of study) enable people to build their own structures of credit accumulation. However, the degree of flexibility varies considerably between systems.

There are two national credit systems – the National Open College Network, and CATS, which is used by many universities. Both use the term 'credit' to describe the numerical weighting of modules that can be accumulated to form an award and transferred between programmes or institutions. Other accreditation systems also allow the flexible accumulation of components or units without necessarily describing them as credits.

When an individual moves from one system to another, there can be problems over whether other accreditation schemes recognise credits because the levels, values and specification of credits are all different. This is a particular problem for adults because they tend to move between systems and can accumulate credits over a number of years. Recognising different forms of accreditation therefore usually involves individual negotiation and the support of guidance and admissions staff. This is time-consuming but a wider, more systematic approach to defining and awarding of credit and for establishing equivalence between credits has not yet been created.

Credit accumulation

Many awards and qualifications are designed so that the separate components achieved and accumulated by learners can be built up over time to obtain a whole award. In credit-based systems, these components can be accumulated as specific credits.

Credit accumulation and transfer

In some accumulation systems, credits gained from a qualification, part-qualification and other learning experiences may be recognised as meeting some or all of the requirements of another award. Learners can then transfer or cash in their credits and progress towards a different award from the original one, or an award in a different institution, without having to repeat assessments and learning.

It is worth noting, however, that there can be problems in some qualifications of transferring old credits or even in using whole qualifications if they are past a certain 'shelf-life' of usefulness.

Level

In addition to different notions of value, there are a number of ways of attributing a level to credits and qualifications. In some institutions' credit schemes these are specified, but in others, they might be implicit. Ideas about whether a credit is at a higher or lower level may be based on:

- the amount of supervision required to perform an occupational role; for example, progression from following routine instructions to self-directed professional activity;
- increasing intellectual and practical autonomy, based on learners being able to apply what s/he has learnt without guidance;
- prerequisites, such as the specific knowledge, skills or qualifications that must form the basis for progression to the next stage; or
- the degree of complexity, or specific context needed to apply knowledge and cognitive skills: this is often evident in university level descriptors.

Many accreditation systems are based on more than one notion of level. For example, NVQs are based largely on required levels of supervision in an occupational role and OCNs on the increasing autonomy of the learner. However, the basis for attributing levels to awards and qualifications is not straightforward and varies considerably between subjects.

Grades

Grades are widely used in assessment and accreditation systems, and have long been associated with selection for higher-level courses and employment where the performance of candidates needs to be differentiated and ranked in some way. The awarding of a grade is based on a desire or need to acknowledge different levels of achievement in relation to the same stage of learning. In some systems, the basis for awarding a grade may be implicit, while in others, grading criteria are made clear to the learners, teachers and examiners. The extent to which learners know what the criteria for assessment and grading are therefore varies considerably from system to system. Sometimes, criteria are provided for teachers and assessors but not made explicit to the learners. In other systems, particularly in university honours degrees, the criteria are frequently neither explicit nor detailed.

Many qualifications base grades on clear assessment criteria. In theory, this approach enables all learners to gain the highest grade, providing they meet the criteria. It is evident that accreditation systems such as

GCSEs, general A-levels or degree programmes are increasingly based on public criteria but do not allow all candidates to gain an A or a first-class grade, however well they do. This reveals a long-running tension in the UK system (especially in England) between criterion and norm-referenced systems and a perception that high levels of mass achievement somehow signify a 'lowering of standards'. Grading is a contentious issue in education and training because it signifies a conflict between a system based on access at any level for anyone who has gained the necessary competence, and the need to ration limited places for progression into higher levels of education, employment and professional training.

Certification

Certification is the formal issuing of a record which indicates that an individual has met the conditions required to award credits or a whole qualification.

When a learner has been assessed and judged to have satisfied the conditions to gain an award, a certificate can be issued by the awarding body or the institution where formal learning has been undertaken. Bodies such as EdExcel, City & Guilds, NCFE and RSA issue their own diplomas or certificates at accredited centres such as FE colleges, adult and community education services, some companies and workplaces, and schools. A college may also offer its own in-house certificates and Open College Networks (OCN) and issue their own credits and certificates for achievement on locally-devised programmes. For honours degrees and post-graduate qualifications in universities, the awarding body is the institution which issues the certificates.

Many work-based training programmes have their own in-house certificates as proof of attendance or skill gained. If these programmes are not part of a formally accredited award, the certificates may still be valuable for including in a portfolio of evidence for the accreditation of learning towards a formal award, such as an NVQ. Terms specifically related to certification are:

Record/Certificate of Achievement

A number of accreditation systems use portfolios or records of achievement as part of their certification. A record of modules gained, the number and level of credits and grades may also contain additional details of achievements, previous qualifications, testimonials and letters of confirmation from employers. A record of achievement can therefore cover a wide range of life and work experience or refer specifically to a particular learning programme. It is either completed at the end of a programme or is the culmination of an ongoing process of reviewing and recording achievement in contributing to the record. The amount of detail provided varies considerably, depending on how the record is used for certification.

Credit Record/Summary

A credit record summarises the titles and numbers of credits grained by a learner. In OCN systems, it includes details of the programme completed and/or learning outcomes achieved.

Profile

Some accreditation systems use a student or learner profile in their accreditation. Like an RoA, it is a summary of achievement, showing the credits gained from an accredited programme of learning. It may also provide details of particular skills and how far the learner has acquired them; some therefore have rating scales to show achievement.

Validation

The terms 'approval' and 'recognition' are used in some qualifications to refer to the process an awarding body uses to validate a centre to run a course that leads to a formal certification. Validation may be carried out either by panels of representatives from an awarding body, professional experts, employers and practitioners, or a representative of the awarding body. In OCNs, recognition panels of tutors and professionals with relevant expertise are used. In universities, academics drawn from an institution seeking to offer a new course and from other universities, together with representatives from colleges, workplaces and students, carry out validation.

Centres and providers usually show how a programme of learning will be organised through a written proposal (sometimes known as a submission) which may cover a range of issues such as resourcing, content, delivery, assessment methods and staff roles, examples of learning assignments and intended learning outcomes. This then forms the basis for procedures in quality assurance and quality control and for internal and external evaluation. Different systems have different requirements and the scope and detail vary, as does the contribution that the process of validation can make to curriculum and professional development for the staff.

In some systems, validation confers approval for an organisation to run a scheme or programme by scrutinising the centre itself rather than requiring a detailed proposal to be made. Validation may be granted for a limited period of time, perhaps subject to renewal after a process of evaluation and review. When used well, it is a powerful form of induction for new staff and professional development for more experienced colleagues.

Franchising

Franchising is the formal granting of a licence or contract to run learning programmes on behalf of centres that have already been validated.

Some universities and colleges offer all or part of their awards through other centres, including workplace organisations. The final award is given on behalf of the awarding body by the centre authorised by the awarding body to run the programme, but the teaching, assessment and learner support is carried out by the staff from the franchised centre.

The same arrangements for validation usually apply to franchised programmes. The centre issuing the franchise is responsible to the awarding body for all aspects of quality assurance, monitoring and staff development.

Moderation

Moderation is a process of evaluation that ensures that the operation of the whole learning programme, including assessment of learners' achievements, continues to meet the recognised (official) standards. In relation to assessment, moderation is used to mediate or moderate differences in judgements between assessors and to ensure that interpretations of criteria are consistent between members of a course team or between centres. The term can therefore describe different activities.

When a course or programme has been validated, some awarding bodies undertake a process of moderation, using external representatives. Moderators review and evaluate the use and quality of learning, facilities and staff roles, as well as the methods of assessment, awarding of grades and levels, and the internal quality assurance of a centre, in conjunction with staff and organisational managers. Moderation is often seen as a supportive contribution to staff and curriculum development but it also has a strong accountability function.

In some systems, moderation focuses much more specifically on processes to ensure that examination papers and marking procedures maintain a certain standard and complexity. External examiners in university programmes, for example, are peers working on similar programmes in another university. They might arbitrate disagreements over marks, compare interpretations of criteria with those in their own and other institutions and ensure consistency between markers in a sample of students' work. They are required to confirm that the standards of work they examine are broadly comparable to those in similar programmes elsewhere. In other systems, such as A-levels, awarding bodies moderate the summative judgements by assessors in one centre by comparing them with assessments in other centres: this is done by postal sampling and regional moderation meetings between awarding body representatives and teachers.

Verification

Verification involves processes to check that assessment in a centre is carried out in accordance with the criteria and formal procedures laid down by the awarding body. However, in the everyday language and activities of teachers and awarding body officials, there is considerable overlap between verification and moderation.

Some awarding bodies use verification in place of, or in addition to, moderation. Verifiers ensure that the centres' assessors adhere to specified standards for assessment and appropriate criteria and that they keep adequate records. The verifier's formal role emphasises assessment procedures and standards of achievement rather than learning processes, the quality of learners' work or staff roles.

The distinction between moderation and verification reflects different notions of quality control and assurance in the various accreditation systems and different traditions. Verification emphasises external monitoring to ensure that the standards for assessment defined and specified by the awarding body are adhered to. Moderation encompasses evaluation of the processes of learning and programme implementation, assessment methods, staffing and resourcing, as well as the end results of assessment.

The degree of scrutiny of learning, assessment and standards is therefore different in each accreditation system. The tone, or ethos, of the verifier's or moderator's approach (and their subsequent report) can also vary between individuals as well as between awarding bodies. The question of which process is appropriate is particularly evident in NVQs, which stress that the mode/duration/place of learning are irrelevant since assessment of competence is the crucial factor. However, many accreditation systems are increasingly combining processes of moderation and verification.

Designing learning programmes for accreditation

Some terms related to the design of programmes leading to accreditation are:

Module

A module is a unit of study and teaching based on an identifiable or assessable part of a learning programme or course. In some accreditation systems, this term is often used interchangeably with 'unit' or 'credit'. In designing a learning programme, modularisation is a way of splitting a whole course into smaller parts (modules) that can be assessed and accredited separately. Some schemes relate module outcomes to the awarding of a credit directly; others offer several credits for a single module.

Modularisation is now widespread in post-16 education and training. Some schemes have a consistent module size, based on hours of learning over a specified time. This uniformity simplifies timetabling and admissions but can lead to reduced flexibility for learners. Schemes with modules of various sizes can accommodate a wide range of programmes, such as short courses. Other modules are based solely on a finite and coherent set of learning outcomes or content. However, learning and assessment are enhanced where attention is paid to offer modules with specific and coherent outcomes that enable learners to make connections between modules and to accumulate skills and knowledge over time.

Modular, unit and credit-based schemes in FE, HE and AE seek to increase the flexibility of education and training programmes by ensuring:
- the assessment and accreditation of prior learning;
- a clearer definition of an individual learner's requirements for accreditation;
- availability of different rates of progress;
- the creation of individualised programmes; and
- a response to changing demand by adding, updating and removing modules from programmes rather than having to redesign whole programmes.

Many providers are anxious to ensure that modularising programmes does not lead to a loss of intellectual or practical coherence. However, there is no agreement on who should decide what combination of learning opportunities is coherent, since learners may choose combinations which make sense to them and their progression, but which teachers and providers see as fragmented and disparate. The role of educational guidance is therefore crucial in assisting learners to make decisions about designing a programme which best suits their needs. In parallel, professional teachers and other organisations who are involved in designing a learning programme need to consider issues of coherence and fragmentation.

Courses

Courses may be long, short, part-time or full-time and are often designed to meet the specifications of content, assessment and accreditation laid down by an awarding body. Traditionally, many qualifications have been linked to courses with the same title for both. This can cause confusion when attempts are made to increase flexibility by separating the two.

Programmes

'Programme' is often used in place of 'course' to stress flexibility and the design of provision to suit specific target groups. It also includes all the learning activity outside classroom contact. A programme can combine modules, assessment methods and access to accreditation in a variety of ways. Programmes can be designed for individual learners and take place in a range of settings. Many people also design their own programme of learning, working independently with books, videos and peers.

Units

The terms module, credit and unit are often used to mean the same thing. A unit may therefore refer to a unit of delivery (module) or a unit of value (credit).

Outcomes

Outcomes are all the gains of learning. This term is sometimes confused with outputs. Outcomes may be specific occupational competences, specified knowledge, cognitive and processing skills acquired through the use and application of knowledge, personal skills such as improved communication, or more intangible things such as increased confidence, motivation and social status. A clear definition of the intended outcomes of a programme enables more conscious and explicit links to be made between assessment and learning methods. However, there are tensions between the drives for transparency and over-specification (see Chapter Five for discussion).

Outputs

Outputs are usually more narrowly defined than outcomes and are therefore easier to assess. Some vocational programmes are funded on the basis of outputs: for example, resources may be allocated to training agencies which achieve agreed targets, usually the attainment of specified awards or admission to specified courses or employment. There is a danger that emphasis on narrow outputs will lead to a distortion of learning programmes by excluding other important outcomes of learning.

3. Choosing the right accreditation system

Institutions may need or want to rationalise the forms of accreditation they offer. Questions intended to provide a checklist for discussing accreditation with the awarding bodies, and for planning accreditation within an organisation or between a number of agencies are offered in Appendix 1.

4. Areas of tension and controversy

Attempts to create parity of esteem between different types of qualifications are dogged by debates about standards, as discussed in Chapter Two. Other questions about the relative merits of different qualifications arise from the UK's unique history of diverse awarding and licensing bodies. In contrast to European countries that either have no national awarding bodies or national qualifications, or where qualifications are designed and regulated solely by government agencies, awarding bodies in the UK are strongly committed to their particular traditions and ethos. In some parts of the education and training system, awarding bodies and accreditation systems have grown organically in response to practitioners' and learners' educational values, for example in adult and community education, where bodies such as the NOCN and NCFE pride themselves on their responsiveness to local needs. In vocational education, bodies such as City & Guilds are proud of their long-running craft traditions where understanding of employers and the demands of a craft are a strong feature of their standing in the qualifications market, both here and overseas.

Awarding bodies also have vested commercial interests in maintaining their presence in the education and training system. For governments intent on standardising assessment systems in order to make them more transparent and accountable, diversity and independent awarding bodies are barriers to central regulation. For the public, employers and learners, diversity is confusing. It might also be argued that diversity obscures debate between different social partners, such as governments, unions, employers and practitioners, about the wider purposes of general and vocational education. This type of debate is more evident in other European countries than in the UK.

The UK's qualification system also offers a very wide range of qualifications and approaches to recognising achievement. Understanding how technical procedures and underlying principles translate into different assessment and certification systems, and where there is overlap or genuine difference, might help institutions, practitioners and learners evaluate the strengths and weaknesses of diverse qualifications. Relating these procedures and principles to some of the political pressures highlighted in earlier chapters might also illuminate the pressures and demands that awarding bodies and government agencies must reconcile.

References and further reading

The major awarding and unitary bodies and QCA offer a wide range of practical guides on assessment and certification, quality assurance and processes associated with moderation and verification. They also run staff development and training events. Details can be found from the following websites:

Assessment and Qualifications Alliance – http://www.aqa.co.uk
EdExcel/BTEC – http://www.edexcel.co.uk
City & Guilds – http://www.city-and-guilds.co.uk
OCR – http://www.ocr.co.uk
National Open College Network – http://www.nocn.co.uk
NCFE – http://www.ncfe.co.uk

CHAPTER 6

DEVELOPING AN ORGANISATIONAL STRATEGY FOR ASSESSMENT

Introduction

This book has discussed techniques, procedures and underlying principles that underpin formative and summative assessment activities in all post-compulsory assessment systems and qualifications. It has also located ideas about assessment practice in a broader, more problematic context of political and social tensions, different goals for education in terms of motivation and autonomy, and competing ideas about knowledge as the basis for learning.

Each chapter in the book has aimed to balance explanations of principles and practices with acknowledgements of some of the deeper tensions and controversies. In a similar vein, this final chapter combines technical advice with questions about the types of motivation and autonomy that assessment activities offered by education and training organisations might promote, both with and for its learners. The chapter suggests, optimistically, that organisations should develop an assessment strategy that meets external demands for assessment while acknowledging gaps between intention and rhetoric and the realities of implementation.

Despite this hopeful aim, there is an ever-present danger that practitioners and institutions under increasing scrutiny and external evaluation will succumb to an instrumental, compliant set of procedures for meeting external targets as painlessly as possible. In addition, the sheer technical complexity and bureaucracy of different assessment, quality assurance and evaluation systems make it tempting to adopt a simplistic approach to rationalising these systems and processes. Further impetus for simple technical injunctions for organisational compliance arise from lack of a coherent rationale for managing educational change (see, for example, Fullan, 1981; 1997).

Although there are barriers to adopting a critical approach to assessment, institutions, course teams and individual teachers could regard the development of an assessment strategy as the basis for at least debating their educational goals and values. Such a debate might be a way to maximise any potential benefits of a strategy for effective assessment and reconciling these values with external pressures. A debate that confronts values and beliefs might, at least, enable practitioners to see why gaps between rhetoric and practice arise in the various assessment systems they use. With these possibilities in mind, this chapter:

- outlines a framework for an assessment strategy;
- explores the implications for staff development in assessment; and
- relates an assessment strategy to the promotion of learners' autonomy and motivation.

1. A framework for an assessment strategy

The stated vision, mission and overall ethos of particular organisations will determine how they organise and offer assessment, and whether they require a policy and strategy for embedding assessment services into learning programmes. A vision statement embodies the guiding values of the institution and the long-term intended purpose of its activities, within its local community or in relation to particular groups and organisations. A mission statement then outlines, in broad or operational terms, what the organisation stands for. Some organisations develop policy statements for particular aspects of their provision, such as access for more adult learners or equal opportunities for all learners.

It is probably self-evident that providers of post-16 education and training face competing missions and imperatives, many of them as political injunctions, such as calls for more specialisation within a defined age group or subject area, versus the demand to provide a wide range of courses and programmes for a diverse local community. Other competing purposes encompass education for economic growth, social inclusion and individual development. However, it might be argued that there is a current lack of vision at government level about the socially transformative purpose of education. Inside an organisation, individuals and course teams are likely to have their own ideas of important educational goals and values. Being clear about mission and values in post-16 education is harder than ever before, but a debate about them might form the basis for recognising gaps between assessment principles, policy and practice.

97

As well as deciding overall policy goals, some organisations have found it useful to identify specific targets for creating better access to assessment and certification for different groups of learners. These targets may be incorporated in development plans, curriculum policy statements and staff development activities. They can all be part of an assessment policy. The process of designing an assessment policy helps an organisation formalise its commitment to providing accessible and flexible 'assessment services'. An assessment policy can also provide the foundation for information given to learners which explains what they can expect from a particular organisation's approach to assessment and how this will be used to enhance their skills as independent learners. If such a statement was offered, it could use the types of motivation and autonomy, discussed in Chapter Five, as the basis for a more precise discussion between learners and practitioners about motivation and autonomy.

An assessment strategy outlines steps that should be taken towards achieving the policy goals embodied in institutional statements. It can be based on a series of detailed objectives and planned targets for the whole organisation or for particular programmes or groups of learners. For example, components of an assessment strategy may include:

- a statement of educational values and mission that embodies ideas about the types of learning, autonomy and motivation that an institution and different courses and programmes within it might develop;
- an organisational audit that might review how effectively different parts of an organisation address different purposes of education and assessment activities;
- a review of particular aspects of assessment, such as initial guidance and diagnostic assessment, perhaps starting with the needs of certain groups such as unemployed adults, and extending eventually to all programmes;
- a requirement for all programmes to specify entry criteria and show how these are assessed, both formatively and summatively;
- a basis for a programme of professional development and training in assessment for all staff;
- a review of how different quality assurance procedures might be harmonised and used productively as an induction and development process for staff taking part.

Stages in designing an assessment strategy

This checklist offers a starting point for organisations, course teams or individual teachers to review, diagnose and evaluate what happens in the institution as the basis for an assessment strategy.

- Examine organisation's overall mission, institutional development plan, curriculum development plans, internal evaluation/review processes (including evaluation by learners), quality assurance procedures in order to identify areas which might require specific policy objectives relating to the organisation of assessment. For example, the intention to widen access for specific groups of learners will affect how assessment is offered to them, while a commitment to promote particular types of motivation and auto-nomy will depend on a particular view of learning and assessment.
- Identify implications for assessment services of institutional plans that aim to develop links with employers, widening community participation or access to higher education.
- Identify or design appropriate policy statements which reflect clearly the organisation's values and assessment philosophy, and derive objectives from them.
- Review current assessment practices:
  a. centralised or co-ordinated across the organisation;
  b. within individual programmes.

  Features of this review might include:
  - location
  - frequency
  - staffing
  - resource allocation
  - methods used.

- Identify areas of good practice and areas for change, including a training needs analysis for developing staff skills and their understanding of assessment, both in relation to techniques and underlying philosophy.
- Design a strategy for implementing policy objectives, with plans for phased change and targets:
  a. across the organisation;
  b. within programme areas.

These could be in relation to overall themes, for example:
- access for adult learners
- work-based learning
- records of achievement or in relation to particular types of assessment service, such as those shown in the model.

- Identify the skills and attributes needed for different assessment activities, taking into account statements of competence required in qualifications for teachers but recognising that these statements tend to take a more technical view of assessment.
- Identify action needed, and staff involvement and/or development needed.
- Plan procedures for monitoring and review, including learner evaluation.
- Identify mechanisms for feeding back information derived from these processes, such as institutional and subject/team development plans.

Tensions and controversies in a technical approach to assessment

In the light of the discussion in Chapter Three about different ideas about knowledge and learning, these activities can promote a positivist view that learning needs can be identified, audited and responded to, or delivered, in a linear, simplistic way. On the other hand, activities might promote a constructivist view that learners' needs and goals, and processes to build these, are amenable to genuine negotiation and dialogue. In heavily prescriptive assessment systems, the design of the specifications and criteria may pull an institution unwittingly towards a positivist model of learning. It is therefore important to consider how much room for manoeuvre there is in different assessment systems.

In discussion of various assessment activities and the skills they demand, the sections below relate each activity to the types of autonomy and motivation they might encourage and to the view of knowledge and learning that might underpin these activities.

2. Developing the assessment skills of staff

Identifying assessment roles, activities and skills

Assessment and quality assurance frameworks can reflect values, purposes and practices as a basis for identifying the diverse roles, skills and qualities that staff in the organisation require to be good assessors.

Assessment may be carried out by:

- staff appointed for a particular role (such as guidance, admissions decisions, initial diagnostic assessment and review of progress);
- staff who carry out a whole range of assessment roles as part of their teaching or workplace supervision and training responsibilities;
- assessment supervisors who oversee the recording of competences for NVQs;
- study supervisors or 'learning managers', who monitor progress and attendance, develop action plans and co-ordinate a learner's record of achievement.

Their roles, and the skills they encompass, are identified in Figure 4. It is important to reiterate the point made in Chapter Five, that simple statements of tasks or activities bely the way that they can reflect either a positivist or constructivist ethos. In addition, activities might promote particular types of motivation or autonomy. For the formative stages of assessment in particular, a clear view is needed on the part of an organisation and its practitioners about whether a positivist or constructivist view is appropriate, and whether they can be combined.

As a starting point for discussion, the activities and tasks are listed in Figure 4 with questions added for each stage of assessment in a learning programme.

Formative and summative assessment activities include:

- enabling learners to recognise their skills and potential and what options are open to them;
- enabling learners to recognise and value their previous experience, learning and achievement;
- tutoring in order to review progress with learners;
- assessing previous learning and achievement as part of selection/ entry decisions;
- certificating prior learning and current competence;
- designing and administering examinations, tests and other assessments; and

- written and oral skills in the discussion of strengths, weaknesses and improvements with students.

An assessment strategy can include specific initiatives to:
- make clear some of the underlying tensions and controversies that assessment both reflects and creates;
- identify the range of staff roles and skills to fulfil the different purposes of assessment;
- explore whether the complex questions identified above at each stage of assessment could be addressed within the institution;
- identify and disseminate the good practice which exists informally on different programmes, and use it as a basis for staff training; and
- provide useful certification for any training or development undertaken by staff where this is required.

A number of organisations have used specific strategies to raise awareness about the importance of assessment through specific strategies. These include:

Management of assessment
- creating 'assessment manager' roles in order to co-ordinate approaches to assessment and certification;
- using cross-organisational groups to review and co-ordinate initiatives and development projects and to disseminate information and identify common links between different initiatives;
- producing a regular bulletin which informs staff about current projects in curriculum development and assessment, particularly when these are based on staff's own research projects.

Staff training and development
- requiring all staff across an institution's entire range of programmes to undertake training in assessment;
- carrying out peer group moderation of colleagues' assessment on different programmes, sharing good practice and allowing tensions and controversies to be raised;
- establishing a network across the organisation to share good practice in portfolio preparation on different programmes and to develop techniques of self/peer assessment, diagnostic and formative assessment;

Figure 5 Tasks and activities

Guidance/Initial Diagnostic Assessment	Entry to Programme	Included in Programme	Certification
• provide materials/facilities to enable learners to identify current competence	• Provide materials/activities (where appropriate) to enable learners to demonstrate skills and/or knowledge	• use valid, reliable and relevant information about learners' progress using sources and formats agreed by the learner	• provide a summary of results and achievement
• refer to other agencies/individuals for information	• provide and explain criteria for entry decisions	• use fair, justifiable interpretations of information to identify learners' needs for further guidance/feedback	• collate information and assessments from relevant individuals and summarise
• assess abilities, skills, aptitude	• use assessments made by other relevant individuals and summarise	• accurately summarise all information and inferences about learners' needs	• write references/testimonials
• assess prior achievement and what opportunities it provides for different progression routes/programmes	• provide positive and clear feedback	• use a variety of types of evidence to assess achievement	• design and provide a range of tests, questions and assignments from which to draw evidence
• summarise assessments made by other relevant individuals	• use a variety of types of evidence to assess achievement	• give constructive feedback	**QUESTIONS**
QUESTIONS		• consider self, peer and ipsative assessment activities	• Do processes for moderation and developing exemplars of work take into account the issues of validity, reliability and fairness raised in Chapter Two?
• Is there scope for genuine negotiation of activities and processes outside the formal specifications of the programme?		• help individuals interpret feedback and review its implications	• Do processes for moderation take into
• To what extent are learners confined to assessment?		• draw up an assessment plan	

Guidance/Initial Diagnostic Assessment	Entry to Programme	Included in Programme	Certification
against pre-defined targets and outcomes?		• help learners identify appropriate evidence	account the tendencies of compensation, bias etc. discussed in Chapter Three?
• Does advice about possible opportunities open to learners reinforce their *introjected* or *external* motivation?		• design and provide a range of tests, questions and assignments from which to draw evidence	• How are the outcomes of final assessment used for formative and summative evaluation within the institution?
• Does discussion encompass previous aspects of a learner's learning 'identity' and experiences (without being intrusive)?		**QUESTIONS**	
• To what extent does discussion enable or encourage learners to identify aspects of learning and interests that might engage them more deeply?		• What tension is there between expectations of validity and reliability in the assessment specifications?	
• Does advice or diagnostic assessment inadvertently reinforce unhelpful ideas about 'fixed ability' or 'intelligence'?		• How do these expectations affect ideas about 'fairness' in practitioners' and students' interpretations of information and evidence about learners' achievements?	
• Does discussion enable learners to start thinking about their autonomy as		• How do expectations about validity and reliability affect the type of evidence that is admissable?	
		• To what does the course, its assessment specifications and practitioners' views about good practice reflect positivist	

Guidance/Initial Diagnostic Assessment	Entry to Programme	Included in Programme	Certification
learners and what this might consist of?		or constructivist images of knowledge and learning? • Where are there opportunities for transaction and negotiation? • Do these opportunities focus on pre-defined targets and outcomes or do they encompass wider ones? • Is feedback on learners' work a one-way process where practitioners expect learners to respond to advice, or are learners actively involved in reflecting on their work? • To what extent is formative assessment more akin to 'coaching to the criteria', and to what extent do practitioners convey expectations of deeper engagement in assessment and learning processes? • What types of motivation and autonomy are being promoted both overtly and implicitly? • Is there scope for self and peer assessment?	

- requiring tutors and lecturers to define learning outcomes and design appropriate assessment across a wide range of accredited and non-accredited programmes;
- providing a weekly cross-institutional staff development and meeting time by timetabling all staff free from formal teaching for two hours.

Other strategies could include:

- co-ordinating administration and registration procedures across an organisation; or
- defining and analysing the skills and qualities needed for successful assessment as part of a training needs analysis.

While it is possible to identify strategies for improving assessment, time to acquire a good understanding of purposes, methods and the various requirements of different qualifications is increasingly at a premium. As this book advocates, time and resources become even more problematic if an organisation attempts to raise awareness about underlying tensions and controversies in assessment. Yet teachers' expertise and commitment are essential for good assessment and these cannot be replaced by attempts to keep refining and controlling 'assessment technology'. This means that attempts to improve practices and techniques need to be related as far as possible to the tensions and controversies that emerge in different assessment models. It also means that practitioners should also be able to identify for themselves what problems are meaningful for them to address with colleagues. Problem-based action research can be particularly effective in enabling teachers to identify meaningful problems they want to address in relation to formative assessment, to try out new approaches with colleagues and to evaluate them critically (see, for example, Swann and Arthurs, 1999; Swann and Ecclestone, 1999; Ecclestone and Hall, 2002).

A carefully designed programme of staff development and training can enable teachers to identify and share good practice, and to clarify which assessment problems are the result of poor design in assessment specifications or learning programmes, lack of skills or more fundamental problems with learners' motivation. A critical approach is crucial because professional expertise in assessment requires skill, knowledge and insight amongst staff, as opposed to merely responding to ever-more detailed guidance and specifications.

3. Promoting learners' autonomy and motivation

Despite the barriers to promoting deeper forms of motivation and autonomy amongst many learners in post-compulsory education, the chart on pages 103–106 indicates activities that might make this goal explicit.

There is growing evidence that many learners adopt strategic, compliant and low-risk approaches to their learning, and that post-16 assessment systems can encourage this as an unanticipated side-effect of transparency and modular approaches (see Torance *et al*, forthcoming; Ecclestone, 2004). Nevertheless, optimism that deeper forms of motivation and autonomy are possible should perhaps be a core professional attribute for teachers! Optimism, together with clearer definitions of types of motivation and autonomy, would enable institutions to review their assessment practices with these goals in mind. For example, evidence of external, introjected and identified motivation might be linked to particular assessment practices such as types of feedback or reviews of progress. Despite the very real pressures on teachers and learners to 'get through' the requirements of summative assessment, there may be opportunities for more imaginative, engaging approaches to assessment that might, in turn, encourage intrinsic and interested motivation, and personal and critical autonomy.

Summary

The technical complexities of assessment, together with growing political pressures for meeting targets and complying with external injunctions for achievement, mean that organisations need to consider how to be more strategic about assessment. This chapter has aimed to show that considering values, principles and some of the complexities of assessment should form part of this strategy.

This is important when professional expertise in assessment requires skill, knowledge and insight among staff as opposed to merely issuing them with ever-more detailed guidance and specifications. Processes that require staff to moderate each others' assessments, to confront problems such as bias and subjectivity and to see quality assurance processes for awarding bodies as opportunities for development can be part of an organisational strategy for assessment that values a professional dialogue about raised in this book.

References and further reading

Discussion of quality assurance and evaluation in education

Fullan, M. (1991) *The New Meaning of Educational Change*. London: Cassell.

Fullan, M. (1993) *Change Forces: Probing the Depths of Educational Reform*. London: Falmer Press.

A critique of the impact of external auditing and targets

Power, M. (1997) *The Audit Society: the Rituals of Verification*. Oxford: Oxford University Press.

Problem-based action research projects that have aimed to improve practitioners' formative assessment practices

Ecclestone, K. and Hall, E. (2002) *Improving Formative Assessment in FE Colleges*, Report to the Learning and Skills Development Agency. Newcastle: University of Newcastle.

Swann, J. and Arthurs, J. (1999) 'Empowering lecturers: a problem-based approach to improve assessment practice' in *Higher Education Review*, 31, 2, 50–74.

Swann, J. and Ecclestone, K. (1999): 'Improving lecturers' formative assessment practice', in Swann, J. and Pratt, J. (eds) (1999) *Improving Education: Realist Approaches to Method and Research*. London: Cassell.

Accounts of assessment systems and their impact on post-compulsory learners

Ecclestone, K. (2002) *Learning autonomy in post-16 education: The politics and practice of formative assessment*, London, Routledge Falmer.

Ecclestone, K. (2004) 'Learning in a comfort zone: cultural and social capital in outcome-based assessment regimes', *Assessment in Education*, 11, 1, 29–47.

Torrance, H., Colley, H., Piper, H., Garrett, D., Ecclestone, K., James, D. (forthcoming) *The impact of post-16 assessment systems on achievements*, London, Learning and Skills Development Agency

Appendix 1

A glossary of assessment terms

The final technical contribution offered in this book is a glossary that summarises the important terms and processes used in assessment and qualification systems.

Accreditation | A formal process leading to the recognition of successful achievement through the granting of an award, or part of an award. Unit accreditation, for example, is offered in some qualifications where learners have successfully achieved the learning outcomes of a unit or module.

ALIS | A-level information system used to collect data about entry qualifications and final achievement in A-level grades.

APEL | Assessment and/or accreditation of prior experiential learning. This enables learners to seek formal recognition (accreditation) of relevant learning from past work and life experience.

APL | Assessment and/or accreditation of prior learning, a generic term that encompasses both the accreditation of prior experiential learning and the accreditation of prior certificated learning.

Assessment | The judgement of evidence of learning and achievement, submitted by learners for a particular purpose.

Attainment targets | The broad objectives outlined in the school National Curriculum that set out the knowledge, skills and understanding pupils must acquire.

CAT

Credit Accumulation and Transfer, the process by which qualifications and past achievements are awarded educational credits so that learners can transfer between courses and programmes.

Certificate

The formal document issued to learners by an awarding or examining body which confirms achievements.

Competence

Statements that delineate and specify the ability to perform job and task functions in a work setting or in simulations.

Core skills

Transferable or 'essential' skills for life and work roles such as application of number, problem-solving, group and team work, communications, information technology and evaluation of own work. Now known as 'key skills'.

Course

A curriculum, usually based on a number of compulsory and optional elements that are studied in a set sequence over a set period of time.

Credit

A measure of the volume and level of learning achieved in a module or discrete element of a course of programme. Credits can be accumulated towards whole qualifications.

Credit accumulation

The process of achieving and certificating separate components of a qualification over a period of time.

Credit transfer

The recognition of credits gained in one qualification system towards some or all of the requirements in a different qualification system.

Criteria   A number of statements that describe how to assess learning outcomes to the required standard and quality of performance.

Criterion   A single statement used for assessing performance that describes one aspect of the quality, or standard, required to achieve learning outcomes to the required level and quality of performance.

Criterion-referenced assessment   A system of assessment that measures learners' achievements against pre-defined external specifications of the required standard, type and context of performance.

Diagnostic assessment   The process of finding out learners' existing strengths and weaknesses in order to offer learning support and guidance about future needs. This can take place before the start of a learning programme and is a crucial part of the teaching and learning process during a programme.

Element of competence   The smallest specification of capability in an NVQ statement of competence. Elements are accumulated to make a unit of competence.

Formative assessment   Assessment designed to diagnose learning needs, barriers to learning and achievements. This enables teachers to give feedback to learners about the quality of their work and future targets. Formative assessment does not contribute to formal grading or final assessment.

Functional analysis   The process of analysing the key purpose and related occupational functions in a broad occupational area.

Guidance

An impartial process that helps learners consider their best options in light of any past experiences and future aspirations. As part of assessment, guidance can be used to help learners assess their prior achievements and consider the next step.

Individual action plan

A set of learning targets and needs negotiated between learners and the organisation providing the learning programme.

Ipsative assessment

Assessment that measures a learner's achievements against criteria determined by her or his previous performance (self-related assessment).

Learning outcomes

Statements of expected achievements that cover practical skills and competencies, knowledge, cognitive and intellectual skills, personal skills, attributes and qualities at different levels of complexity and across different contexts and situations. These outcomes can be specified in detail or in general statements and are usually accompanied by criteria for assessing them.

Moderation

The process of comparing and confirming assessment decisions and judgements between assessors in order to standardise assessment decisions. This can be carried out between teachers and by awarding and examining bodies, and when there is an overlap between moderation and verification.

Moderator

An external assessor appointed by an awarding or examining body to monitor standards achieved on a set of vocational courses or programmes.

Module

A unit of learning and assessment that is usually free-standing and can therefore be taken separately or in conjunction with other modules.

National Record of Achievement	A national system for recording achievement from school through life and encompassing different qualifications.
NOCN	National Open College Network, an accrediting and awarding body for adult education programmes and many of the 'access to higher education' courses.
Norm-referenced assessment	A system of assessment that measures learners' performance and ascribes a standard to it by comparing it to the performance of other candidates in the same cohort.
NVQs	National Vocational Qualifications are accredited by the QCA and offered by a range of awarding bodies which cover a wide range of occupational areas and jobs.
Occupational standards	Descriptions of types and levels of competence in a job role which is established by Sector Skills Councils (ex-Lead Bodies) in an occupational area in order to create NVQs and other aspects of work-based training.
Performance criteria	The specific criteria that establish the range, scope and quality of performance candidates must show in order to gain elements and units of competence in an NVQ.
Portfolio	A collection of evidence of achievement such as assignments, projects and artefacts made by learners in learning programmes or from other life and work experiences which can be submitted for formal assessment and accreditation.
Progression	The development and accumulation of skills and achievements through successive learning opportunities and the opportunity to move on to another related stage of learning.

Quality assurance The processes and procedures developed by organisations and awarding bodies to ensure the quality of learning programmes, assessment and accreditation during a course or qualification.

Record of achievement A document that records formal and informal achievements.

Reliability Assessment that is designed to ensure that the same range of results gained by learners could be reproduced in a different cohort of learners who are deemed to have similar abilities. Assessment designed for reliability aims to enable assessors to standardise their judgements against those of other assessors.

Summative assessment The formal assessment process that enables assessors and verifiers from awarding bodies to judge evidence of achievement submitted by learners in order to determine a final result or grade in a module or unit, or for a whole qualification.

Unit of competence a component of an NVQ that is broken down into elements of competence. A unit represents a discrete aspect of competence and can be accredited separately and accumulated over time towards a full NVQ.

Validity Assessment that is designed to accurately measure a range of learning outcomes. Assessment designed for validity aims to enable different interested parties to infer that these outcomes have been achieved and that learners could reproduce them in other similar situations in future.

Verification The process of internal and external monitoring carried out by awarding bodies and institutions to ensure that assessment and accreditation procedures are being correctly and systematically adhered to and that standards are being achieved against set criteria. Guidelines for verification in NVQs and GNVQs are issued by the awarding bodies.

Work-based assessment The measurement of performance in the workplace, usually by a work-based assessor.

Index